Virtual Learning

The impact of ICT on the way
young people work and learn

JOHN P. CUTHELL
The University of Huddersfield, UK

Ashgate

Aldershot • Burlington USA • Singapore • Sydney

Published by
Ashgate Publishing Limited
Gower House
Croft Road
Aldershot
Hants GU11 3HR
England

Ashgate Publishing Company
131 Main Street
Burlington, VT 05401-5600 USA

Ashgate website: http://www.ashgate.com

British Library Cataloguing in Publication Data
Cuthell, John P.
    Virtual learning : the impact of ICT on the way young
    people work and learn. - (Monitoring change in education)
    1.Computers and children 2.Education - Data processing
    I.Title
    371.3'34

Library of Congress Control Number: 2001089777

ISBN 0 7546 1776 9

Printed in Great Britain by
Antony Rowe Ltd, Chippenham, Wiltshire

Contents

List of Figures

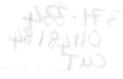

List of Tables

Introduction

For almost twenty years successive governments have realised the importance of computers and computing and made significant investment in schools. The latest initiative, the National Grid for Learning, seeks to place online learning facilities at the heart of the curriculum for both teachers and students, and use it as a vehicle for Life Long Learning. School communities – students, their parents and their teachers – have struggled to manage technological change when resources, particularly those of time, have been stretched by the curricular and administrative changes they have had to implement.

The impact of ICT in the classroom transforms management, organisation and conventional pedagogical approaches. Many teachers still struggle with the demands of ICT in the classroom: the ICT training programme provided by the New Opportunities Fund (NOF) aims to provide the skills and theoretical framework within which educational praxis can absorb these changes. ICT is seen as an integral part of each strand of the National Curriculum, and the performance of teachers is to be judged on their ability to integrate ICT within their teaching and their students' learning.

From the mid 1990s, however, a significant number of students have gained access to a personal computer at home. The ways in which they have learned to use the machines, and the uses to which they are put, are shaped more by personal experience and input from their peers than by their schools. The programs they use, the ways in which they learn and the work they create mean that the education system struggles to meet the demands and expectations of these young people. What follows, of course, is that those who do not have this technology at home are doubly disadvantaged if their schools and teachers cannot compensate.

During this period these issues have been investigated by the author, and this book is based on several years' research into patterns of computer ownership and use among young people. A six-year longitudinal study of some 1800 students at a comprehensive school in West Yorkshire provided the data from which the results were drawn. Student work was examined during this period, and students themselves commented on the ways in which computers had changed their work. Teacher use and teacher attitudes were also examined. The results clearly demonstrate the disparity between student computer ownership and use and that of their teachers.

The ways in which those people with computers learn how to use them have shaped their assumptions and expectations of what it is to learn. They are less likely to accept conventional pedagogical approaches as appropriate to them.   The patterns of learning experienced by young people are at variance with the assumptions and expectations of their teachers, with profound implications for the education system.

When the investigation began, much then-current research focused on curriculum and institutional uses of ICT.   Underwood and Underwood (1990) examined the whole-school use of ICT, Watson (1993) examined the impact of ICT on children's achievements and Wood (1998) evaluated Independent Learning Systems (ILS).   Papert's work on LOGO has focused on cognitive gains from the use of that program.   Turkle (1995) studied the impact of online communities and computer use among post-adolescent students.

What was missing from the literature was a study that examined the effects of home computer use among young people, and the ways in which this impacted on the education system. This study shows how the learning patterns of young people are now often shaped by the ways in which they use a range of technological tools: games machines and mobile 'phones, but particularly computers.   The expectations about learning and work which these young people bring to their classrooms are in conflict with those of the school and their teachers.   The learning patterns and learning gains need to be understood if they are to be capitalised upon by the education system. Without that understanding the efforts of schools, and the talents of students, may well be undermined. The citizens of the twenty first century are being taught in classrooms of the twentieth century whose praxis is shaped by the 1870 Education Act.

Computers present students with powerful tools for learning. Young people who use them have been set free from conventional expectations of learning. This raises profound issues for the educational system of the new century. This book examines and details these issues. To date, there has been little exploration of them. Teachers and schools may find an alternative to conventional curricular approaches to learning. Parents will gain an understanding of the learning processes that their children's computer use supports. Young people who read it may recognise what they are doing, and learn how to apply the insights.

1   The context to the research

Background

> As the use of a new technology changes human practices, our ways of speaking about that technology change our language and our understanding. This new way of speaking in turn creates changes in the world we construct.
>
> (Winograd and Flores, 1988, p.6.)

From 1984 to 1986 I worked in Dammam for the Saudi Arabian Language Institutes, and purchased an IBM-compatible computer for the office. Within a week the Palestinian secretary had compiled a database of all the clients, set up a spreadsheet to track income and expenditure, and was enthusiastically using a word-processor to generate correspondence. He taught himself, with the help of phone calls to friends and the occasional use of the manual.   Six months later the routine operations of the office had been transformed, and Ibrahim, the secretary, was able to make suggestions as to the ways in which the administration of the Institute could be changed. The technology had empowered him.   When I looked at other companies with which I came in contact I found, to a greater or lesser degree, the same process.

Many of the clerical workers in company offices had been recruited from Jordan, the Philippines, South-East Asia and the Indian sub-continent. They arrived to find a workplace very different from those which they had left.   All the offices had installed computers, and the staff were expected to use them.   When their contracts had finished many of these bought computers to take home and use in their own businesses.   All to whom I spoke believed that these machines would transform their family businesses, and their lives.   They saw computers as a means of giving them access to a technological revolution which would plug them into the developed world.

It was not simply that the utilisation of computers for office tasks had increased their efficiency: that tasks could be undertaken more swiftly and easily.   The more profound change was that these workers could envisage different ways of doing things.   Their style of working could change.

British schools

In 1987 I returned to work in comprehensive schools in West Yorkshire. The Local Education Authority had chosen to equip all schools with Acorn microcomputers (usually referred to as 'BBC computers', after the promotional television programme). I found that students and teachers were using Acorn BBC computers for very different tasks to those I had seen in use in the Middle East: here they were used as aids for learning mathematics or science; as a way of presenting final drafts of writing, or, in Business Studies, studying databases. Many enthusiastic teachers were struggling to fit computer use into existing schemes of work, or were teaching students about computers. I found very few examples of teachers - or students - using computers to transform the ways in which they worked, and the outcomes they produced. Computers were predominantly seen as external to the school process of learning and work, and to be used for specific purposes.

I considered that two aspects were central to the ways in which computers should be integrated into the education process. The first was how students could undertake work using a new tool. The second was whether this tool fundamentally changed the artefacts which were produced. These issues were rarely the focus of the way in which teachers used computers with their students.

The articles which I read on educational computing, and the courses run for teachers by the schools' advisory service, were more concerned with the skills which were needed in order to use the computers with students. The dominant approach was for teachers to learn how to use programs to achieve particular outcomes relating to their curriculum, and then to teach the students how to use the programs in order to achieve those outcomes. Students would use computers to learn how to produce grid references in Geography; to calculate the nutritional composition of meals in Food Technology or for word prediction in English using cloze exercises.

Much of the then-current research literature was devoted to the examination of ways in which the use of specific programs could reinforce and extend aspects of the curriculum and the learning process. (The occasional papers published by the Information Technology and Education Programme, (1986-88) and InTER (1988-90) Information Technology in Education Research Programme (ed. Lewis, R. 1986-90); University of Maryland: Human-Computer Interaction Laboratory; Northwestern University: The Institute for the Learning Sciences.)

Much of the software I encountered in schools had been produced by enthusiastic teachers, whose approach utilised game formats in which students were awarded scores to signify success. The paradigm of Computer Assisted Learning was dominant: short sessions on the computer for specific groups of students to reinforce the normal curriculum.

My professional reservations were that such a policy presented computers and their use as something which had to be taught and applied in specific ways, and that the students' role was no different from that in any other subject. Computers in schools were objects about which students had to be taught. Their use was seen in terms of skills which had to be learned before they could be applied. The power and independence which I had seen in colleagues in the Middle East, when computers were adopted with no formal instruction, suggested that this was not the most educationally beneficial application of the technology. However, it was an efficient way to utilize scarce resources. In such a context it was far easier to use computers to teach students about them, rather than allow students to use them.

Extending the technology

During the next three years the school at which I was working invested significant sums in extending computer provision. A whole-school network was put in place, new software was purchased, and new syllabuses adopted in Business Studies which provided opportunities for independent student work. Staff training sessions were organised to introduce teachers to the new possibilities.

Paradoxically, the increase in investment and the commitment to staff development did not seem to produce a corresponding increase in the use of computers across the curriculum. Where a department adopted computers as part of their work with students, computer work was added as additional units within the syllabus, rather than to transform student work. The Mathematics department scheduled a unit of work involving computers for each student in years seven and eight; the English department added a word processing unit.

There was no increase in the numbers of staff using computers as an integral part of work with the students. Those teachers who had embraced computers when they were introduced continued to develop their work. Most, though, saw them as irrelevant to their subject. The weekly timetables and booking sheets for the IT rooms would be used by the handful of staff who attended the IT Support and Development Group meetings. Other colleagues were reluctant to be persuaded to use the facilities. They would cite curriculum pressures that prevented them from taking classes to use the facilities, the unreliability of the machines or the difficulties of managing students in an unfamiliar environment.

Transformations

By 1990, however, the situation changed when a significant minority of students started to have access to computers at home that ran industry-standard software and which had printers. These computers were significantly different from those which students used for games playing or programming. In the majority of cases they were business machines which had been replaced, written off by the accountants and sold to employees for a nominal sum. The coursework these students produced in a range of subjects not only reflected the skills they had acquired at home, but also enabled them to produce documents that many referred to as 'real'. What was interesting was the fact that many students used databases, spreadsheets and graphics to support and illustrate points that they were making in their writing.

One consequence of this was that students were able to analyse data and view a number of graphical representations of it with very little effort. This ability to cycle through different charts and to view the data in different ways meant that students were able to decide which data sets were significant. In turn, this meant that their writing became more analytical: the ability to generate and view a range of data representations meant that causal links could be tracked easily. The length of time which the process would have taken had the students created the graphs manually would have prevented them from contemplating the task.

Another, possibly more significant, consequence was that these students began to plan and organize their work in terms of the technology to which they had access. They would pressure their teachers to use school facilities: students without access to a home computer would add to the demand. Some teachers realised that their lack of expertise could be compensated for by involving IT-literate students as mentors to others within the class.

Investigating the changes

During the next three years a growing number of students with whom I came in contact spoke enthusiastically about the computers they had at home, the ways in which they used them and how these compared with the limitations of the school resources. By 1994 I decided to survey the whole school population to see whether this was indeed the case, or whether I was projecting the enthusiasm of a few students into an unsustainable generality. I also decided to survey students as to why they used computers: I wanted their perceptions.

The investigation of what the students did with computers, and an exploration of their reasons for doing it, required a methodology that would accommodate a range of responses and generate a typology. Previous research I had undertaken in student perceptions of genre in television, and the ways in which they used soap operas such as *Neighbours* and *Coronation Street*, suggested that a Uses and Gratifications typology (McQuail, 1987) might provide an appropriate way in which to approach the data. It was analyzed using a modification of McQuail's Taxonomy of Gratifications.

The first of the whole-school surveys was conducted in February 1995, the second in February 1996, the third in February 1997 and the final survey in February 1999. The data on home ownership of computers confirmed the initial supposition, that a significant number of students had access to these. Whilst many students had access to an IBM-compatible computer running a Windows operating system, in 1995 there was a heterogeneous mix of machines cited by students as computers. Many younger students listed their games machines: others, older systems.

With each survey the impact of the PC on students and their work became more pronounced. The introduction of multimedia machines gave students access to a range of reference material: the last survey showed the impact of the Internet on students' working patterns. At the time of the final survey a computer using a Windows operating system – sometimes referred to as the 'wintel hegemony' - had become synonymous with the term 'computer' for all students.

The effects

A consequence of this is that students with a machine at home have shifted the site of production for their work from school to home: they feel more in control of their work, they don't have to compete for scarce resources at school, and they can use a newer system which they have configured for themselves.

The rate of change in the computer market and the emergence of computers as consumer goods made it difficult to ground this study in educational research. Much of the background evidence, therefore, was drawn from industry sources, where resources and funding were such that there was an immediacy to the data difficult to achieve in other circumstances. Surveys from manufacturers during this period (ICL, Olivetti, 1997, Microsoft, 1997) and consultancies (McKinsey and Co., 1997) supported the penetration of computers into the domestic market (Longman PC ownership survey, 1997). The McKinsey survey speculated as to ways in which home ownership of computers was likely to change the nature of compulsory education. When Microsoft provided their own Internet service it was described as 'a private education'. For many young people the concepts of computers, Microsoft programs, knowledge and education were becoming inextricably linked. Knowledge and learning were presented as commodities, to be purchased, and replaced when they need updating.

The implications

When computers were introduced in schools in the United Kingdom the computers to which children had access at home were often either machines used for generating programs, or dedicated games machines. Schools used a range of computers, from Acorn/BBC, through Commodore, Dragon and Research Machines, to those assembled by staff and students. A variety of operating systems, software and hardware could be found within those workplaces that had adopted microcomputers.

As 086 IBM PCs with Intel chips and MS-DOS operating systems became standardised in business, so they had an impact on students. With the increasingly rapid changes in technology companies adopted a faster write-down in their accounting policies, and 'obsolete' machines found their way into homes. When Windows became the de facto standard, students who acquired these machines suddenly found themselves with an extremely powerful machine to learn and use. These computers were increasingly identified by students with the adult world of business, and were therefore regarded as 'real'.

By 1995 PCs were promoted as consumer goods. Programs were distributed on the covers of magazines, and students found that they were able to learn how to use these and combine them with other programs in order to produce work for school. For the first time, a significant percentage of students in this country found that they could learn how to use something that most of the adults in their lives could not. These students worked out for themselves how programs were used: each of them learned slightly differently, and they traded this information at school.

Students are now continually experimenting with new programs, new applications and new technology. They are in a process of continual learning, which they control. They see that much of the computer technology which they have to use at school is older than theirs, with more limited software. More importantly, there is a level of institutional control that is imposed on their use of it that conflicts with their understanding of how the technology could be used.

The quotation with which this thesis opens suggests a social-constructivist approach to knowledge and learning.

> As the use of a new technology changes human practices, our ways of speaking about that technology change our language and our understanding. This new way of speaking in turn creates changes in the world we construct.

Winograd and Flores (1988) suggest that the changes which a new technology produces in our practice, the ways in which we work, should also effect a change in the ways in which we speak about our ways of working. If the ways in which we speak about something change, then the ways in which we understand things will also undergo a change, which should, in turn, change the ways in which we perceive the world and construct meanings from it.

If Winograd and Flores are correct, then these changes in student practices should effect changes in the language and understanding of students. These should then produce changes in the world they construct.

The research perspective

The research on which this thesis is predicated was conducted over a period of six academic years. It involved all the students in the school. The longitudinal surveys were undertaken in tutor time, and the sample size for each survey varied according to a number of factors: reliability of the school buses, small-group activities during tutor time and student absence. Nevertheless, between 1200 and 1300 students were surveyed during each phase of the research – up to 70% of the school population of 1800. A comparative survey compared these students and those from another comprehensive school in the city. The only comparable large-scale survey with which comparison could be made during this period was the Ultralab survey of emergent capabilities, which was single-phase.

Other surveys involved selected year groups: Years 7-10 and 12. These investigated student attitudes towards using computers for work and the perceived benefits; the ways in which they perceived the Mind and how it worked; the ways in which they thought they learned. Teacher surveys were also undertaken during the research: those from the school were surveyed during the student surveys: those from other schools in the local authority at other times.

The perspective was essentially ethnographic, in that it examined the ways in which young people and their teachers used and made sense of constantly changing technology. This work is therefore about changing perceptions, expectations and conceptions, where knowledge and understanding are constructed with each new action and utterance, and where learning is just-in-time.

Much of the empirical evidence collected during this period is located in the appendices. Some are summaries for this research and for colleagues: others were conference papers or articles for journals. All present snapshots of a process.

I was constantly surprised at the changes and developments the research revealed: my expectations were often subverted.

2 Methodologies, concepts and framing perspectives

Introduction

The use of computers by young people has been subject to many research perspectives. A considerable body of this research has focused on the ways in which computers could enhance or transform learning and schooling (Papert, 1980; Clements and Gullo, 1984; Watson, 1987; Schostak, 1988; The InTER Programme, 1988-93; Underwood and Underwood, 1990; Somekh and Davis, 1991, 1997; Dwyer, 1994; Cox, 1997). Other research has focused on the ways in which computers are used (Winograd and Flores, 1988; Schank et al., Institute for the Learning Sciences research programmes; Shneiderman et al., Human-Computer Interaction Laboratory). At the same time there has been concern about the impact of computer use on young people (Turkle, 1995; Levinson, 1997; Sanger et al., 1997; Griffith et al., 1999). The use of information and communications technologies within schools has become a political issue (Blair, 1998; OFSTED 1998). The ways in which the effects of computers on young people have been studied have many parallels with attitudes towards the effects of television on the young. The subject, therefore, is complex and requires a multi-layered analysis.

This study has been informed by a number of perspectives, rather than being grounded in one particular methodology. They form part of my own theoretical framework and have enabled me to interrogate the data from more than one viewpoint. They throw spotlights on the data, which was collected over a five-year period and subject to many different types of analysis. Some of these theoretical perspectives have shaped my praxis for most of my professional life: the centrality of language in the ways in which young people construct their own learning; the importance of tools to augment intellectual processes; the belief that young people can articulate their reasons for working and learning. Others have been explored during the course of the study. None of them, however, forms the underpinning theory upon which the study is based. Instead this is more a matter of the refinement of the concepts that have been with me and emerge from the difficulty of taking understanding further by the application of existing methodologies.

The research methodology

The research was designed to generate information about three areas: the level of ownership and use of computers across the school population; young people's reasons for using computers; and young people's understanding of computers and their capabilities. The initial vehicle for data collection was a response sheet which students were invited to complete. It contained two tables, one headed 'Home', the other, 'School'. Each table contained three sections: at the top of each was a prompt. I use computers for... ; because... ; type.   The first assumption was that quantitative data would be collected, although the approach was different from those who try to isolate every possible variable. The openness of the response sheet was such that there were a number of unexpected results (see Appendix 2 and Appendix 4).

I wanted to provide a format which would allow as wide a range of responses as possible within these three areas. The first survey generated a rich collection of data: most students provided a commentary on the information they entered. This serendipitous conjunction of quantitative and qualitative data was unexpected.   As a result, the format was retained for all the subsequent surveys.

Data collation and analysis

Collating and analysing the data initially posed problems of organisation. Before the first survey was carried out a considerable amount of time had been spent with colleagues discussing options. These centred on questions which students should be required to ask, the ways in which these could be analysed and the uses to which they would be put. The consensus was that a structured data collection sheet should be used which provided students with a series of options to choose. This would have enabled data to be analysed much more easily.

Despite the ease of collation and analysis, however, the format would have limited personal or idiosyncratic responses. This approach was not used: previous research I had carried out into young peoples uses of television suggested that the most productive responses were those which I would never have included in a structured questionnaire. The format of open responses was used: it would provide essential quantitative data and allow its qualitative analysis.

The data generated from the first two prompts was useful, instructive and consistent. They provided quantitative data related to each tutor group and each year group, broken down by gender. This data could be expressed in percentage terms, providing a picture of ownership across each cohort. The approach was retained in subsequent surveys: it provided a clear, sharp focus; there was nothing to hide, it was easy to report.

The quantitative data relating to the level of ownership changed over time. The longitudinal nature of the study meant that presentation of the data in percentage terms provided a clear picture of this change. The data was also used by year teams and curriculum managers across the school to inform their decisions, and its presentation as percentages enabled comparisons to be made both across, and between, year groups.

Data from the 'because' section was analysed in terms of item frequency, collated and grouped. Again, it was expressed in terms of percentages for each response and each cohort. The findings were detailed and consistent. Students went to great lengths to explain how and why they used computers.

Other data collections invited students to write letters or provide explanations. The ability to extract qualitative data from what was ostensibly a quantitative survey, in that students proved willing to offer a great deal of information, provided extremely rich content. This too could be presented in a range of ways.

The only personal information students were asked to provide on the response sheet was their year group and gender. Despite this, a number of students provided their names and indicated that they would be interested in following up the survey. They were more than willing to volunteer the information. They had clearly reflected on the ways in which they used computers, and the part the machines played in their lives, and wished to express their interest. This contrasts with the assumptions in some research that students would be reluctant witnesses, and that a structured survey sheet requiring minimal input from young people is the most effective method of collecting data.

This personal and unsolicited response from students enabled the content to be validated through random conversations – a form of convenience sampling. These conversations took place in their tutor rooms, when students were using IT facilities (particularly during lunch times), and when moving through the school outside lessons. The most valuable of these conversations occurred when students would approach me and initiate discussion about using computers, knowing that I was conducting research.

In a very few cases a response sheet was suspect or highly ambiguous, and was therefore counted as a zero response. Examples of these occurred when 'I don't know' was entered for gender, or 'Sex' was entered after the 'I use computers for ...' prompt. These examples were, however, extremely rare.

During the six-year survey student coursework was also analysed to establish the ways in which it was produced using ICT, and teachers were asked to comment on the effects of ICT on work and marks.

Media and audiences

During the course of this research, a number of concerns emerged in the media about the use of computers and their effects on young people. These ranged from the moral panic over access to computer pornography, through VDU-induced epilepsy and the perils of Repetitive Strain Injury to the activities of teenaged hackers. As access to the Internet increased, so did journalistic worries over the apparent availability online of anarchist handbooks, pre-written essays and dissertations and, most of all, pornography. All of these worries mirrored the theme of Media Effects, predicated on the question of what use of the media did to its audience. In the case of computers and young people two concerns have become conflated: the first, that the unlimited use of computers will affect the young people who use them; the second, that the apparent availability of 'unsuitable' material available at the click of a mouse will cause young people to seek it out.

Uses and gratifications theory

A contrast to the assumptions of 'Media Effects' theory is that of 'Uses and Gratifications'. A Uses and Gratifications approach is posited on the assumption that an audience consists of active individuals who do things with the media – they are autonomous consumers (McQuail, 1987). These uses are held to gratify the needs of the individuals. The approach is, from one perspective, democratic, in that it gives a voice to the people who use the media. There are, however, a number of reservations about the methodology (Severin and Tankard, 1997). These are based on the assumption that 'ordinary' individuals are not aware of their real reasons for making media choices: the data has to be explicated by researchers. In this study, however, we found that students were able to articulate their reasons for using ICT, both on the survey response forms, in letters they wrote advising on the purchase of computers, and on the ways in which they thought that they learned.

Caution has to be exercised when implementing a 'Uses and Gratifications' analysis. The validity of this approach is dependent upon respondents giving an accurate account of their reasons for using media. Uses and Gratifications theory is also individualistic, in contrast with earlier positivist instrumental approaches. The social and economic context of media production (and use) is often ignored by both researchers and respondents. This is particularly apposite when the media under investigation is that of computers. Another limitation is that the ways in which meanings are constructed through media use, and the ways in which these frame later responses, do not lend themselves to an investigation of this type. The reality is that the rapid development of technology and its instability, together with the increasing patterns of ownership, have meant that young people have been anything other than passive consumers.

The final criticism of a Uses and Gratifications approach that collects responses is that it is essentially consumerist and non-theoretical, vague in key concepts, and nothing more than a data-collecting strategy (Severin and Tankard, 1997). All that respondents are providing is a list of preferences: all that researchers are doing is accepting those preferences and providing a set of league tables. What we have here in this research is more subtle: we are making no assumptions.

These reservations may be held to have some validity if respondents are considered as no other than passive consumers of media. However, the advent of interactive computer media (programs, multimedia and the Internet) means that individuals adopt a far more proactive attitude towards what, when and why they will use it. We cannot hold on to simplistic stimulus-response models.

Despite these reservations the Uses and Gratifications approach provided an appropriate framework within which to organise the data collected in response to 'because...'. The categories of Surveillance, Personal Identity, Personal Relationships and Diversion were transferred from media use to computer use very easily, with student responses often including a number of categories according to context. The audience survey provided valuable data which formed the basis for the research into the effects of computer use. A more complex analysis of the relationship between young people and Information and Communications Technology was then possible. Information and Communications Technology can be regarded as a medium: this analogy is borne out in the responses of the students.

This ease of use was not without problems, however. One of the Gratifications identified by McQuail was the sub-set Personal Identity. This provided the largest set of responses, with students identifying computer use and computer knowledge as an integral part of their identity. They saw the use and knowledge of computers as providing access to the 'real' adult work, and the skills and concepts which they were acquiring as providing them with an advantage over those who did not possess them. At the same time, the ability to navigate the complexities of computer games gave status within their peer group. The question arose as to whether this constituted a legitimate sub-set, or whether it was simply a convenient catch-all. One response to such heavy weighting of Personal Identity would be to discount it as too broad and general a category. However, it was decided that this should be retained, because it represented an important strand to the way in which students regarded computers, and the way in which they positioned themselves in relation to their development and their world.

The use of this approach to the data enabled me to identify the ways in which students thought about, and used, their computers. It provided a perspective that enabled additional areas to be explored during the next four years.

The researcher as observer and participant

Throughout the survey, I attempted to provide students with ways in which they could explain their actions and motivations in their own words. This process often involved a level of practical reasoning that enabled them to explain that which they would otherwise take for granted. The research was concerned with identifying the individual experiences of, and interactions with, computers by the students, and the ways in which they conceptualised these. Above all, I have been concerned with the context of their computer use.

At the same time as I was collecting data from the students I was also extending my own use and understanding of computers, a process which often informed my interpretation of student data. I was both a participant and an observer: a participant in learning about the extent and implications of computer use, both by myself and with students. I was also a participant in the student learning that took place. I was therefore both participant and observer in the 'way of life' of the students with their computers, as well as their activities and the educational contexts. What I was concerned with was the ways in which young people made sense of the computer technology they used, and the ways in which they incorporated it into and managed their lives. This approach could be seen as drawing on ethnographic traditions of research. It was the integration of computers into their own lives that became increasingly important as the research progressed. The starting point had been simply how the students approached computers, at home and at school. This emphasis shifted to why students handled computers in the ways in which they did.

Symbols

The Graphical User Interface that has become the de facto standard provides students with icons and symbols through which to work. My approach to their uses of this computer interface, and the ways in which students construct documents for their coursework and websites, is informed by my readings of semiotics. This 'science of signs', in which communication, through the signifier (the sign), results in what is signified (the message) has had a long influence from Saussure (1915) onwards. The advertising that surrounds these young people provides a constant lesson in this to them.

Semiotic ideas have since permeated much of the way we ground ourselves in (post)modern life: our reading of television advertisements, magazine photographs and modern buildings is predicated on signs and messages. Work as diverse as those of Barthes (1957; 1982; 1987), Eco (1976; 1986) and Hodge and Tripp (1986) have informed the readings of student work in these surveys. Work undertaken with students has also indicated ways in which young people read and deconstruct the media: from Cullingford (1984) on children and television; through Buckingham (1996) on children's emotional responses to television; to Robinson (1997) on the ways in which children read both print and television. Young people are sophisticated media consumers. This sophistication is transferred to the medium of computers, through which they can apply creativity.

The layout of a computer desktop is a perfect example of interactive semiotics: the icons signify not only their function, but what can be achieved through them. All the transactions the user wishes to undertake can be conducted at a virtual level. New icons can be created for the desktop which will generate further messages: the computer will carry them out.

Cyborgs

As man-machine artefacts, cyborgs embrace our concepts of humanity and artificiality, intelligence and programming, thought and instructions, gender and androgyny. The development of medical technology has introduced a cyborg element into people wearing contact lenses or pacemakers; biotechnology and genetic modification brings awareness of our hold over the creation of life. Hollywood uses cyborgs in its depiction of distopian warnings of technologies out of control and societies in decline. Perhaps the most productive intellectual use of the cyborg metaphor is the way it has been used as a tool to interrogate questions of gender and social identity in our network of social relationships, from labour and economics, through biotechnologies to ethics (Haraway, 1985). Here, the cyborg has the possibility of a hybrid being, not subject to the constraints of social, political and gendered identity.

The cyborg perspective provides a productive focus for interrogating society. Web sites such as The CyberStudies Resources Site (http://ccwf.cc.utexas.edu/ ~glik/index.html) provide access to a constantly mutating set of memes.

The way in which students in these surveys have used the concept is influenced by media drawing on a range of science fiction: Terminator; RoboCop; Blade Runner, and is very often tongue-in-cheek. However, they do visualise computers as enhancing their own capability. This is more than a fashionable trope: it frames all of their perceptions about the ways in which the technology has become embedded in their lives. Technology can be seen both in Nature and as Nature.

My reading of the term, and the way in which it has been applied throughout this study, is its original one: a man-machine interface which performs automatic routine checks and monitoring, enabling the human to create, think, feel and explore. (Clynes and Kline, 1960) The relationship between the young person and the technology used is iterative: feedback from the program, the machine and online sources sets her free from the mundane to create artefacts that would otherwise not be possible. Chapter 6 explores these themes.

Building things: the DIY approach

Levi Strauss (1962; 1996) uses the term 'bricolage' to identify a science of the concrete in which structures are improvised to devise a system of meaning from given material. Levi Strauss draws on elements of semiotics in his analysis of the ways in which structures of meaning are constructed from 'what is at hand'. The concept is applied here to the ways in which young people create their own artefacts and systems of understanding from materials which they find to hand on, and through, their computers.

Computers as the means of production

The term 'capital' is used in this study in two ways. The first is in the sense of real capital, having a money value and constituting a productive asset. This relates to the computers, associated hardware and software to which the students have access at home. The second is that developed by Bourdieu (1986; 1993) of cultural capital and symbolic power which, through the education system, reproduced social and class relations. The symbols, language and culture of the dominant group constitute a hegemony of social characteristics which serve to differentiate the groups: the education system reinforces that differentiation. Cultural capital is often represented by cultural goods, artefacts that signify membership of the dominant group. The acquisition, understanding and use of computers constituted an important aspect of cultural capital for the young people during the five years of the study.

Hegemony

I have used the term Hegemony to describe the way in which a set of practices and assumptions come to dominate the praxis and thinking of a group. In this sense it is not a 'world view' in the Gramscian framing, (unless one applies it to the current dominance of Microsoft's operating systems and software and Intel's processors) but rather a set of assumptions shared by students and staff in our school. These assumptions are regarded as 'common-sense' and taken for granted.

The assumptions about computers that constitute such a hegemony have been imposed by students: in this sense, they represent the 'dominant class', and their teachers have come to accept them as 'common sense'. The first assumption is that personal computers are synonymous with Intel-based PCs running Microsoft programs. The second is the assumption that assignments set for examination coursework should be word-processed, include tables, charts and other graphics and be set out in business-style report formats. The final assumption is the trickle-down effect for students in Years 7 through 9 that, for work to be classed as 'good' that it too should be presented in the same way as that of Years 10 and 11.

Computers, then, represent the site of struggle between many students and teachers in the school. The imbalance between student ownership and that of teachers, and the differing skill levels of each group, has enabled students to hold the dominant position and determine much of the discourse. (See Chapter 5; Appendix 1; Appendix 2.)

3   Some research perspectives

The research evidence

When I started my reading for this research, the literature on young people and computer use could be loosely categorised as having three perspectives. The first was the impact of computers on motivation, work practices and classroom pedagogy. The second perspective focused on the effects of computer use on cognition. The third perspective was that of the evaluation of predominantly technical issues connected with software, multimedia and the human-computer interface.

Many of these themes are, however, intertwined. The issues are complex because the rate of technological change is such that it is difficult to compare like with like; because young computer users are themselves in the process of developmental change; because they form part of a peer learning community that mediates these effects and because of their expectations that, although nothing will work perfectly, a 'best fit' can be achieved and hardware and software forced to work. The complex information with which I was dealing was reminiscent of aspects of Chaos Theory.

Research themes

The ESRC Information and Technology Programme (1986-90) investigated specific issues involving the use of computers in education: the Information Technology in Education Research Programme (InTER) of 1988-93 established a multi-disciplinary approach to four research themes. The five-year programme investigated:

- collaborative learning;
- the development of basic concepts in mathematics and science;
- tools for exploratory learning and simulations;
- the identification and evaluation of learning gains achieved through the uses of information technology.

The programme investigated the effectiveness of computers in specific domains. Three questions were posed relating to the information technology resources which they had:

- what do people do?;
- what do they want to do?;
- what can they do?

The four research themes, and the questions posed, are as pertinent today as they were when the programme was initiated. Indeed, the research literature to date has been built on this foundation. The subjects of research that formed the basis for initial studies of the educational use of computers have been extended and developed. The effectiveness of multimedia in education has been examined in depth, as has the use of Computer Assisted Learning in a number of disciplines. (Hodges and Sasnett, 1990; Dwyer, 1994.)

The assumptions that inform these studies developed when computers were not the aspirational consumer good they became in the mid-1990s. Indeed, for most children, access to computers was provided through educational institutions, and teachers administered their use. School was, for the majority of children in North America and Europe, the only place where they could be used.

Affective factors

Other studies have focused on the effect of young people's computer use on interactions within the classroom. Collaborative learning, where computers were a scarce and shared resource, introduced a range of outcomes different from those within a classroom where individual learning was the norm (Somekh, 1986, in Schostak, 1988). The Pupil Autonomy in Learning with Microcomputers Project (PALM) of 1988-90 (Somekh and Davis, 1997) focused on the ways in which computers enhanced pupils' learning, functioning as intellectual tools, to support a range of mental functions.

A significant finding (present throughout this study) was that many teachers regarded the computer as a 'neutral tool' and over-valued the presentational aspect of computer work. If the computer was a 'neutral tool' then it would simply facilitate the production of work. The improved presentational aspect of the work was therefore to be expected. Teachers would no longer have to battle with poor handwriting; there would be fewer surface errors; students would include tables and charts in their work; in short, students would publish their work.

Other teachers found themselves suffering from 'informational overload' when they were no longer able to control the information flow to which children had access through ICT. When information sources accessible to students were predominantly print-based, the teacher could identify school resources and make a best guess as to the provenance of others. Not only that, but students could be guided to resources. With Internet access and CD-ROM resources at home, teachers find it increasingly difficult to assess unattributed work.

This disjunction between teacher and student perceptions was examined by Monteith (1996), who investigated the ways in which IT was used at home and at school. She identified the possibility of learning being accessed differently at home and at school, with consequent problems for schools, and for those without access to a computer at home.

Computers as agents of change

Literature on the impact of computers on education can either focus on such macro issues as motivation, changing classroom pedagogy and cognitive enhancement, or micro issues such as the effect of computers in specific curricular domains. The advent of the microcomputer has challenged the privileged position of the school as the gatekeeper of knowledge for young people. This opens up macro issues that question the place of education within a social structure. Micro issues examine such factors as the effectiveness of computer-assisted learning programs, or the impact of shared computer access on collaborative classroom settings.

Challenges to the structures of education

Schostak (1988) identified the potential for change that computers offered the education system, in that pupils had, for the first time, the possibility to author their own course. He saw control of the process of information handling, in an environment that was tightly controlled, as creating a state of independence for pupils, in that information became a process, the products of which had been constructed. Computers carried a virus that had the potential to create an 'intelligent community' of users, 'augmenting the intellectual power of the individual over that of the political community', but which also heralded the end of secondary education.

Despite these assumptions the culture and organisation of schools persists. What changes have occurred have been in ways that were not forecast. This study, however, sees subtle but profound shifts in attitudes amongst the students themselves, both in the ways in which work is undertaken and the ways in which learning is constructed and situated.

Schools as the gatekeepers of knowledge

Before the increased power and ubiquity of multimedia computing enabled this vision to become reality, however, the introduction of the National Curriculum and changes in teacher education limited the space for such developments. With so much of the curriculum prescribed the time available for experiment and development was curtailed. Nevertheless, a student with a multimedia computer, CD-ROM reference disks, internet access and a range of web sites could be said to have the power to construct their own knowledge and education.

At the same time, evidence was emerging that indicated that computers had a transformational effect on pedagogy and had the possibility for education to fulfil the aims of those who saw it as a way of fostering the autonomy of the individual and enabling each to reach her full potential (Somekh and Davis, 1991).

This view was contrasted with the formal perceptions of many within the structures of the state system, who felt that the tide had finally turned against what were disparagingly termed 'progressive' theories of education. The role of teacher was increasingly seen as that of instructor; and the process as one of filling empty vessels, rather than as facilitating learning and kindling fires of enthusiasm in the construction of knowledge. The contradiction between organisational expectations and student experience became stronger during the course of this study.

The same debate was taking place among those involved with the production of educational computer programs. Watson (1987) examined the tensions inherent between programmers and teachers, who often had a 'fuzzy' approach to the ways in which they wanted the programs to work. Such teachers felt that the impact of computers in the curriculum, particularly as they were used within Humanities subjects, provided space for a constructivist approach.

Changing classroom pedagogy

The 1990 study of Underwood and Underwood surveyed and summarised current practice involving microcomputers in school. They identified the two perspectives which shaped attitudes: 'formal' and 'progressive'.

Computers and the formal approach to education

The first perspective could be seen as 'formal' or 'traditional', in that learning is seen as the reception of knowledge and the learner is a recipient of information. This approach has much in common with the behaviourist tradition: computers are therefore additional tools through which teachers and the educational process could achieve existing aims and objectives, whilst at the same time providing keyboard familiarity and IT awareness.

Computer programs to support specific curricular aims through exercises and drills provided one set of examples: the Acorn/BBC initiative spawned a generation of teacher-programmers who saw Computer Based Learning as a panacea for otherwise boring routines to reinforce the curriculum. The conventions of spelling and punctuation, routine mathematical operations and other such aspects of the teaching process were entrusted to programs that adopted the format and conventions of computer games. Other programs enabled students to practise compass bearings, giving grid references or producing time lines. The Micro in the Classroom became an addition to the Non Teaching Assistant.

The eventual introduction of Independent Learning Systems (ILS) provided a neatly packaged solution to this approach to learning. Students would sit at computer terminals, log on to their personally tailored program, complete the work and, with appropriate feedback, emerge successful. The students sit in front of their own terminal. In many cases they wear headphones for aural feedback. They work their way through the materials, make changes and receive a score at the end. Their teachers can access their learning logs and monitor progress. This Behaviorist stimulus-response approach of many of the Independent Learning Systems is quantifiable and works in that each student is removed from many of the variables of a normal classroom learning environment.

Computers and the progressive approach to education

The second perspective drew on the 'progressive' approach to education, grounded in cognitive and constructivist approaches which saw knowledge as a social and intellectual construct, with the learner as an active participant. The use of computers in schools was therefore a way of changing both the process and the product of the education system. An early advocate of using microcomputers in this way was Papert (1981). His book Mindstorms saw the use of computers, and what he terms microworlds, as a way of enhancing and transforming the cognitive capacities of children. Papert's perspectives are firmly grounded in Piagetian Developmental Psychology: LOGO, the programming language which he developed, was seen as a way in which children's cognitive development can be developed through simulations in microworlds.

LOGO and cognition

A number of subsequent studies (Clements and Gullo, 1984; Hughes and Macleod, 1986; Klahr and Carver, 1988) appeared to support these claims. The use of LOGO was seen as a way in which thinking skills could be developed and transferred to other situations.

To date, there is a considerable body of research literature which has evaluated the impact of LOGO use on children's mathematical and problem-solving skills, and a smaller set that examines the impact on affective factors such as motivation and socialisation. Clements and Meredith (1997) cite 85 research papers on the uses of LOGO in schools. Of these, 78 examine the use of LOGO in the teaching and learning of mathematics. Seven studies evaluate the effects of LOGO on attitudes: among them are investigations into social-emotional development (Clements and Nastasi, 1985), self belief and achievement (Blumenthal, 1986; Emihovitch and Miller, 1988; Horner and Maddux, 1985), and social and cognitive interactions (Clements and Nastasi, 1988). The studies suggest that success in using LOGO as part of the classroom environment promotes self-esteem and enhances development. Collaborative learning and problem-solving are also enhanced (Kapa, 1999).

These studies have not, however, examined the ways in which these skills may be transferred to other aspects of independent computer use. The focus is very much that of a teacher-led educational process (Schostak, 1988). Part of this study examines student perceptions of learning, and the ways in which computer use and skills are transferred.

Changing the practitioners

Preston and Harris (1993) examined the impact of computers in schools on teachers' professional practice, and their need for in-service training. This was at a time when changes in funding for local education authority support services were beginning to affect the provision of such training. At precisely the same time developments in computer technology and software increased the need and demand for such training.

The consequences of this could be seen in the OFSTED review of Secondary Education 1993-97 (1998), which identified pupils' IT capability as poor in 2 in 5 schools, and not as well developed as other key skills. Many students and schools focused only on basic applications such as word-processing. The pedagogy of IT as a subject was described as 'still poorly developed', with too much of a focus on the teaching of mechanical IT skills at the expense of higher-order capabilities. Staff development in Information Technology was most frequently judged by OFSTED to be unsatisfactory.

The document 'Excellence in Schools. White Paper on standards in education' (1997) was, in part, a response to many of these concerns. It proposed, among other things, the creation of the National Grid for Learning and suggested that within ten years ICT would have permeated every aspect of learning. New teachers were to be trained to be fully ICT literate, and existing teachers were to be retrained using National Lottery funding. (The New Opportunities Fund.) All schools, colleges and libraries would be connected to the Internet at the lowest possible call rate, a Virtual Teachers Centre would be established and home learning via the Internet would be developed.

Whilst the DfEE was simultaneously advocating ICT for its transformative powers and prescribing, testing and inspecting what would be done it was questionable whether school-based initiatives would be enough in themselves to effect change. Cox (1997), however, had identified the motivational aspects of ICT use for students and for teachers (Preston, Cox and Cox, 2000) when both teachers and students were able to use the computers to transform the ways in which they worked. Preston and Cox found that both student and teacher autonomy, together with access to the technology, were key to the successful use of ICT and its impact on learning. This complements research that shows that successful integration of ICT into teaching is also dependant on the fit between the software and the teacher's pedagogical practices (Watson, 1993). These findings were supported in this study by responses from teachers.

Moral panics and social perspectives

A distopian response to the Utopian vision of the White Paper takes as its perspective the misuses of technology by young people. The activities of hackers led to the Computer Misuse Act (1990), whilst the image of young people out of control on the information highways of the world has led to concerns about the corruption of minors by computer-based pornography (Merchant, 1994), on-line anarchist handbooks and the addictive potential of interactive systems (Griffiths, 1994). The image of socially inept young males becoming addicted to the Internet has also been raised (Turkle, 1995; Griffiths, Miller, Gillespie and Sparrow, 1999). Whilst the ethical issues involved in children's attitudes towards concepts such as copyright and software piracy still remain to be explored, British newspapers have followed the lead of the American press in suggesting that the Web offers a cornucopia for cheating undergraduates. More reflective commentators have worried about the socially divisive effects of the 'information rich' and 'information poor'.

There are many parallels between these perspectives and studies of the uses which children make of television. What is lacking, as with so many studies of children and technology, is the voice of the children themselves, and what they feel they are enabled to do by computers and information systems. A recent study examined the uses made of computer games by children in primary schools in East Anglia, and contrasted this with ways in which computers were used in their schools (Sanger et al., 1997). They found that many teachers in the study were ill at ease with the technology; that in many cases the classroom computer was at the periphery of activities, both physically and educationally, and that its main use was as a tool for producing neat copies of work. The ways in which children used computers at home were seen by both teachers and children as fundamentally different from school uses. This is also confirmed in this study.

Turkle (1995) has examined the effects of computer use on individuals in the United States, but her perspective is more that of the psycho-social effects of computer use, rather than on the transformations that young people are empowered to make within their learning. Turkle sees the main impact of computer use, especially with the Internet, as impacting on questions of identity and social placement, offering '…new models of Mind and a new medium on which to project our ideas and fantasies. … We are learning to live in virtual worlds' (p. 9). She describes computers as 'objects to think with' (p. 48).

Effects of computers as 'objects to think with'

Winograd and Flores (1988) on computers, cognition, language and Mind, provide a useful focus for an examination of transactions and processes. Whilst the underlying approach of their work is that of the role of language in constructing knowledge, they characterise the faculty of understanding as pattern recognition, which involves representations and procedures. The work of the neurophysiologist Maturana is central to their thesis of the changes in understanding brought about by the uses of new technology. The concept of plasticity, (Maturana 1970; 1980) and structural coupling within the cognitive system, posits a dynamic interaction between interactions and the structure of the interactive system. As the domain of interactions is modified, so is the structure of the interactive system. In this way the use of computers, and the language representations which their use involves, modifies traditional domains of interactions in the cognitive developmental process associated with children and school. Winograd and Flores' use of Maturana's work provides a rationale for the thesis that the use of computers changes children's thinking processes. Their work complements that of Papert, whose initial work explored the effects of LOGO both as a program and an environment for learning.

Other such programmes of research, most notably based in North America at the Human-Computer Interaction Laboratory at the University of Maryland. (Shneiderman et al., 1989-98) and The Institute for the Learning Sciences at Northwestern University (Schank et al., 1990-97), have evaluated the effectiveness of specific computer tools as a way of enhancing the quality and type of learning.

Technology as a metaphor

Information technology and information processing have been employed by philosophers engaged in the debate between Cartesian dualists and neurophysiologists. A number of writers have examined the way in which the Mind is constructed as a metaphor: objects and processes in our environment are used to construct the metaphors in order that we can understand the Mind. The trend can be seen in cognitive development and symbolic information processing, (McShane, 1991) and on understanding data handling and computer procedures as a way of understanding ourselves. (Leiber, 1991) Parallel with this debate is the reification of computers in the discourse of teachers, students and the Government, in which computers assume an active identity and a super-ordinate role. The

National Grid for Learning and the Supergrid for Learning are seen as a way of avoiding

> ... a generation of the information poor ... to be productive, Britain needs to become a knowledge driven economy ...   (Blair, 1998.)

The view of education as providing the skills infrastructure for a '...productive...knowledge driven economy' is predicated on the assumption that knowledge and information will be readily accessible and shared among society's members. Information and Communications Technology is seen as neutral, with an autonomous, independent status relative to the structures of society and the actors within it. ICT is also seen as a benign contrast to the old, polluting smokestack industries. The post-industrial world is clean; it heralds the end of commuting; it brings the world of knowledge to the desktop of each individual.

The twin themes that have informed so much of the research on computers, young people and schools – computer as tool; computer as transformer – have here intertwined themselves to produce a thread for the future. The supposition is that the thread will bind us into the web, e-commerce, e-learning and the wired economy. The hope is that unlike Theseus, we will not find ourselves in the dark, at the end of a piece of string with a monster heading towards us.

4 Research into patterns of computer use: Surveys, 1994-1999

The school context

The comprehensive school at which I worked in West Yorkshire served the communities to the north east of Leeds. It was attended by some 1800 students, was non-selective and offered access and progression to the full ability range from Year 7 to Year 13.

The research context

From the outset of the Computers in Schools initiative in 1983/84 the school had developed an IT policy based on a number of stand-alone machines. By 1987 a classroom had been networked with Acorn Master 128 computers. During the following year the networking was extended to cover further classrooms, with older machines used as printer and teletext servers. Students throughout the school had access to the network during lunch times for their own work. When the Acorn Archimedes computer was introduced additional facilities were provided on a departmental basis. For a long time, therefore, the students had been familiar with a networked computer environment.

In 1990 four teaching staff established a school-based training company to develop new learning technologies. This initiative was funded by the Department of Trade and Industry, and resulted in a body of expertise being developed in the production and applications of Hypertext, CD-ROM and online information retrieval.

Developments in GCSE Business and Information Studies, and vocational courses such as BTec and GNVQ, demanded a range of software applications (often referred to as 'business standard') that offered the students transferable skills. It was decided that the school should provide a mixed economy for the students: a Novell network (funded by the training company) supporting IBM-compatible PCs was installed, whilst Archimedes machines were used where appropriate. As the Acorn

Master machines reached the end of their economic life they were replaced by networked PCs.

The result was a whole-school PC network covering each department, equipped with fifteen PCs, appropriate printers and with access to a scanner; clusters of PCs in the library work area, a careers-specific network linked to a printer, and clusters of PCs, linked to a printer, in the Sixth Form Common Room.   There was open student access to computer facilities and the Internet outside lesson time.   Students also used video-conferencing facilities within parts of the curriculum.

Networked PCs with Internet access were also available for staff use in offices and work areas.   Individual departments also used (old) stand-alone PCs as teaching and learning aids.   The school administrative system ran on a separate network utilising software common to the LEA (SIMS: Schools Information Management System), with terminals installed in each year office.

The school curriculum policy was for information technology to be regarded as cross-curricular, rather than as Information Technology, a specifically timetabled subject.

The research problem

The school had made a significant investment in information technology over a period of ten years, with some staff committed to innovative uses. The school and its company had won a number of awards to develop innovative learning technologies.   By many indicators, both in the extent of ICT technology to which students had access, and the projects in which a significant number of staff were engaged, the school could be considered to be more IT literate than many others.   One would expect there to be an appropriate curricular impact on classroom activities and teaching and learning styles.

The reality of the learning experience of information technology across Key Stages 3 and 4 was, however, at best patchy; at worst deficient. National Curriculum requirements did not appear to be met if the measure was work undertaken within school.   Work produced by those students who had a computer at home, on the other hand, suggested there was expertise and a depth of experience which was not recognised within the school.

There appeared to be a growing disjunction between National Curriculum expectations, cross-curricular experience and students' personal computer use.   It was possible to determine, from the allocation of teachers on a student's timetable, the likelihood of that student receiving the information technology input deemed appropriate by the National Curriculum. Despite this, students produced computer-based work in order to meet assignment requirements, in many cases despite, rather than because of, their teachers' instructions. They appeared to have access to a capital base at home, and to possess and use skills which they had not been taught at school.

At the same time, anecdotal evidence from teachers in department and year meetings during the academic year 1994-95 suggested that many students preferred to work on their computers at home, rather than those at school. They reported that such students were using this as a reason not to engage in work during classes, and cited it as a negative impact of computers on the school process.

No objective evidence existed, however, for the extent to, or ways in which, computers were used. It was decided to survey both students and staff to determine the uses to which computers were put, identify patterns and suggest ways in which curricular outcomes could be improved. The survey was repeated during the academic years 1995-96, 1996-97 and 1998-99.

Methodology

In the spring term of 1995 the first survey of home computer ownership and use among the students was undertaken. Students in every tutor group were asked to indicate their access to, and use of, computers at home and school. The response sheets contained spaces for students to comment in detail, should they wish. 1331 students responded: some 74% of the total school population. The shortfall reflects student absence, the pressure of activities during morning tutor time and the priority placed on the exercise by the form tutor.

The initial survey was followed by a more detailed investigation of responses from Years 9, 10 and 12, in which students were asked to comment on the extent to which they thought it worth having a computer at home for work. Detailed student responses formed the basis for interviews. Comments from students are used to illustrate points throughout this section.

The ownership and uses survey was repeated during the spring term of 1996, 1997 and 1999. Sample sizes ranged from 1256 to 1380. The size and extent of the samples, therefore, suggest that conclusions drawn from the data can be considered valid.   The spring term was chosen to include those students who received a computer as a present for Christmas.

1995 findings

The first survey showed the following pattern:

Table 4.1: Students with a computer at home: the uses to which it is put, 1995

Total number of respondents in the survey		Number of respondents with a computer at home	
Gender	Number	Work and games	Games only
Male	674	418 (62%)	229 (34%)
Female	657	355 (54%)	170 (26%)
Total	1331	773 (58%)	399 (30%)

58% of all respondents (773 students) either owned a computer, or had access to one at home.

58% of the students (773) who completed the sample stated that they had a computer at home that they used for work.

35% of the students (466) stated that they had access to a PC with a Windows operating system.

In some cases responses cited specific software applications: Microsoft Works (the integrated package used across the school PC platform); Microsoft Office and its components, or Lotus SmartSuite and its components.   The significance of this is that in Spring 1995 more than 30% of students had access to the same technology as used in the business world.   These students utilized the same programs.   They used the same exemplars - grounded in the context of American business - for document production.   None of the programs cited by students had been produced for the education market, other than those for Acorn computers.

The ways in which students classified their hardware produced a spectrum of age and utility which correlated very closely with uses.   For IBM-compatible PC users, older students referred to their machines in more technical terms - 286; 386; 486-SX or -DX - than younger students, who simply cited PC, or Acorn. In Years 7-9 students would state that they used their computers for writing, drawing or graphs, whereas in Years 10-13 the software would be stated - Works ('...for everything...': Year 11 girl); AmiPro or Excel - and the uses related to specific coursework assignments. The implication of these statements was that the students making them had a sophisticated understanding of their computers and software applications.

The perspective of students at the school was that Acorn Archimedes computers were promoted as the standard machine for education. The policy of the local education authority, for instance, had been to develop IT programmes and expertise around this standard, and its funding and supply policies have reflected that. The Educational Information Technology Centre provided in-service courses based on Acorn computers for teachers. Despite this, students who were Archimedes owners and users constituted only 3% of the school total, and of the BBC Acorn a mere 0.4%. It was clear from these figures that the acquisition of a computer for home use was hardly influenced by the machines in use at school. This compared with Macintosh ownership of 1% and Amstrad PCW use of 4%, neither of which machines were used in the school.

Student ownership and use of the Commodore Amiga, on the other hand, was 15%. In 1995 the Amiga constituted the most problematic machine for student use. The marketing and advertising for the computer was targeted at the games market, but the added value was perceived to be the software bundles that enabled 'real' work to be done. Advertising for the Commodore Amiga was consumer oriented: computer games magazines were the primary information source for many young people, although outlets such as Dixons and Currys featured the machines in their catalogues. Of possibly more significance, however, was their supply through Argos and mail order catalogues.

The focus on work-related software had proved to be an important strategy when students were negotiating their purchase with parents. All Amiga users cited 'assignments' or 'work for school' as one of their uses. A number, however, added that there were compatibility problems with file transfer or printing between home and school. The games capacity of these machines had been their greatest attraction. The additional effort involved in using the machines productively proved too great for many. Students from Year 11 onwards volunteered that they would have been better advised to purchase a PC.

1996 findings

The survey was repeated a year later, in Spring 1996, to determine whether any trends could be identified. The results were compared with those of Spring 1995, with a specific focus on Intel/Windows-based machines. They showed a significant shift in home ownership of PCs.

Table 4.2: Home ownership of Personal Computers (IBM compatible), 1995-96

Year Group	Spring 1995	Spring 1996
Year 7	26%	42%
Year 8	31%	43%
Year 9	35%	41%
Year 10	42%	55%
Year 11	46%	56%
Year 12/13	49%	62%
Whole school, as % of respondents	35%	49%

Figure 4.1 maps these changes.

Figure 4.1: Home ownership of Personal Computers, 1995-96

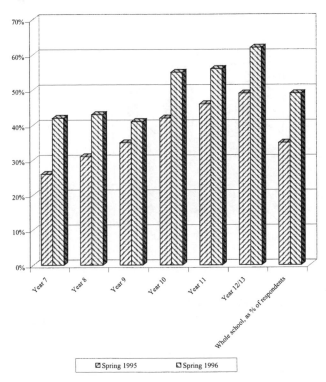

The significance of the shift can be seen when the growth in ownership across each student cohort of Key Stage 3 and 4 is examined.

Table 4.3: Increase in ownership across student cohort

	Spring 1995		Spring 1996	
(Year 7)	26%	$\Rightarrow$	43%	(Year 8)
(Year 8)	31%	$\Rightarrow$	41%	(Year 9)
(Year 9)	35%	$\Rightarrow$	55%	(Year 10)
(Year 10)	42%	$\Rightarrow$	56%	(Year 11)

Figure 4.2: Increase in ownership over one year

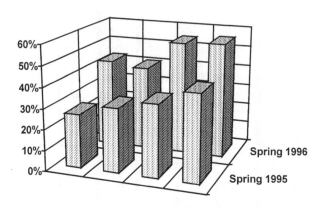

As this growth in ownership of machines continues, then there is a corresponding growth in the concept of ownership of work. The site of production for many students has been relocated from school, (which is associated with limited access to facilities - time and resources - and, above all, teacher direction) to home.

Research comparisons 1996-97

During the academic year 1996-97 the survey was undertaken in a city school in the local education authority. The school was chosen to provide additional data. It is an inner city school and the student population could be considered less economically privileged than those at our school. Many of the students are drawn from ethnic minority groups. Our school, on the other hand, has a catchment area more representative of the overall population, taking in commuter villages and housing estates to the north-east of the city.

Methodology

The student survey utilised the same open response format of previous surveys, following the prompts:

I use computers for... because... Computer type.

Student surveys

Students at both schools were surveyed during the tutor period at the beginning of school. Those at the City Comprehensive School were surveyed during the first week of December, 1996. Data was obtained from 283 students: 43% of the school enrolment (658). Students at Boston Spa Comprehensive School were surveyed during January 1997. Data was obtained from 1380 students: 77% of the school enrolment (1787). The disparity between the number of students surveyed and the number on roll was due to absence, lateness or other activities that removed them from their group during tutor time. The scope of the survey, however, suggests that the data represented the upper and lower levels of computer ownership during this period. City School was surveyed before Christmas; our school after: this in itself would heighten the differences between the data.

The results in the following tables are only for home ownership of personal computers. There were limited responses from students from both schools for Acorn, Amiga, Atari BBC, and Mac computers used at home for work, and a greater number of responses for computers such as Nintendo, SEGA and Sony that were only used for games. The focus of the investigation, however, was on those computers that can be classified as belonging to the Intel/Microsoft duopoly (Wintel): using MS-DOS and Windows operating systems.

1997 findings

Table 4.4: Home ownership of Personal Computers, 1997

Year Group	BSCS	CCS
Year 7	47%	16%
Year 8	52%	11%
Year 9	55%	16%
Year 10	62%	22%
Year 11	67%	32%
Year 12/13	72%	38%
Whole school	59%	20%

BSCS: Boston Spa Comprehensive School
CCS: City Comprehensive School

What these figures demonstrate is an increase in student ownership from Year 10 onwards. The disparity between BSCS and CCS, however, can be contextualised by comparing results from the first survey carried out at BSCS in February 1995 with that undertaken at CCS in December 1996.

Table 4.5: Home ownership of Personal Computers (IBM compatible): disparities

Year Group	BSCS February 1995	CCS December 1996
Year 7	26%	16%
Year 8	31%	11%
Year 9	35%	16%
Year 10	42%	22%
Year 11	46%	32%
Year 12/13	49%	38%
Whole school	35%	20%

Two possible interpretations can be placed on these figures:

either students at CCS are two years behind those at BSCS in terms of acquiring PCs, and that individual access to machines will increase during the coming years (with an expected increase in ownership after the Christmas holiday);

or the figures reflect the social and economic differences within the population.

The ownership of home PCs, the use of them for schoolwork, the acquisition of skills and concepts represented by them and the value placed on these by society represent the economic and cultural capital of the Information Society. The divisions highlighted in these results reflect groups that have been termed 'Information Rich' and 'Information Poor' (Blair, 1998).

If students see the possession of a computer as empowering them, both in terms of ease of production and quality of production of school work, and if this translates into enhanced grades for examination coursework, then the issue here is simple. Schools have the responsibility to ensure that all students have equal access to the technology that creates those opportunities. The demands of the labour market suggest that students who leave education without the concepts and accompanying skills developed through constant computer use and application will be economically and socially disadvantaged.

Extending ownership: 1997–99

The Spring 1997 survey was then compared with the results from that undertaken in Spring 1999. The most significant growth in ownership occurred between these years. Comparison can be made with previous years.

Table 4.6: Ownership growth at Boston Spa Comprehensive School, 1995-99

Year Group	Spring 1995	Spring 1996	Spring 1997	Spring 1999
Year 7	26%	42%	47%	77%
Year 8	31%	43%	52%	80%
Year 9	35%	41%	55%	78%
Year 10	42%	55%	62%	84%
Year 11	46%	56%	67%	84%
Year 12/13	49%	62%	72%	85%
Whole school	35%	49%	59%	81%

Figure 4.3: Ownership growth, 1995-99

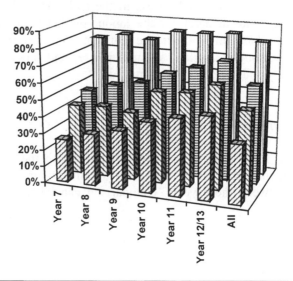

☑Spring 1995 ☒Spring 1996 ☰Spring 1997 ▥Spring 1999

As the student cohort moves through the school, so the incidence of ownership increases. Students in Year 7 when the first survey was undertaken were in Year 11 for the final sample. Table 4.7 illustrates the increase in ownership.

Table 4.7: Cross-year comparisons

Spring 1995		Spring 1996		Spring 1997		Spring 1999	
Year 7	26%	Year 8	43%	Year 9	55%	Year 11	84%
Year 8	31%	Year 9	41%	Year 10	62%	Year 12	85%
Year 9	35%	Year 10	55%	Year 11	67%	Year 13	
Year 10	42%	Year 11	56%	Year 12	72%		

Factors affecting the growth in ownership

The acquisition of a high-value good is based on the assumption that its purchase will produce a number of benefits. As part of the research, students were asked to write a letter to a friend, who had asked whether it was worth obtaining a computer for school work. Their comments illustrate their perceptions that ownership of a computer has enhanced their work, and indicate factors that young people consider important.

Student attitudes to computers

> The only bad point of doing your homework on a computer is that you tend to find you have a lot more homework as you cannot write things up in lesson. ... PS Make sure you get some good games etc. Doom2 is an excellent game....
>
> (Boy, Year 10.)

Here the student has identified an increasingly common pattern. Students are increasingly regarding the classroom environment as a place in which work is not 'written up'. If a lot more homework is produced at home this has significant implications for students, in terms of the time they go to bed, the materials they bring to school and, possibly most importantly, the fact that no-one is seen to 'work' in class.

> the writing is smaller when you print it out ... you have to write more so you get a better mark.
>
> (Girl, Year 9.)

If work rate was traditionally measured in terms of handwritten pages of an exercise book, then the shift to 12-point word-processing on A4 pages is significant. Less sophisticated students try to compensate by

using larger fonts, or increasing the size of the header and footer.   Others
'…write more…'.

These student comments illustrate themes identified at the outset of the research.   The first is that students are now doing work at home that they would otherwise have done at school.   The second is that many students find that using a computer tends to objectify their work.   What is produced is seen as an artefact, and evaluated as such: it correlates with the students' sense of 'neatness'.   Improvements to the artefact are related to the rewards of the task.

As one student in the survey commented,

> Now I use my computer for all the work I do apart from Maths and things like that.   I can draw on my computer, make music, listen to music, write stories, look up words to find a meaning for it like a dictionary, print out any work I want for homework.   I think it makes homework a lot easier because of all the different programs.
>
> (Boy, Year 9.)

For this student the computer was integrated not only with the process of work and the products which were produced, but also the environment of work. The mechanical aspects of work, such as printing out, the functional aspects, such as looking up the meanings of words, the creative – drawing, writing stories and the recreational – listening to music, are brought together.   Another student described the other changes produced by his computer:

> Computers can make homework need a lot more time, even if you're very good at using them, because you end up spending a lot of time tweaking your work.   The end product can look very good, especially with expert use.   Spell checks and automatic language aids such as Thesaurus help your writing.   Computers with reference software, such as "Encarta" are great for research. AmiPro2 is the best word processor/d.t.p. program in the world. Apart from AmiPro3.   You can also sharpen up your brains playing games such as Tetris and Doom.
>
> (Boy, Year 10.)

In this example we can observe a double effect.   The student not only spends more time 'tweaking' the work, but also works harder at the process to become an 'expert'.   Work is no longer limited to the recall of input from teachers, but extended through 'research'.   A constant theme of students is the way in which work and research are combined through the availability of CD-ROM reference works.   Involvement with the task of homework was seen as a part of personal and intellectual development:

research, improving work and developing games-playing skills - 'sharpen up your brains' - are part of the same process.

The ease of production of artefacts enabled young people to see themselves as moving beyond previous limits imposed by motor skills, time and performative competence.

> On my PC we have AmiPro, for a word-processing package and Lotus 1-2-3 as a spreadsheet program. I use the computer to word process assignments as my handwriting is very messy. Also because it is easy to change things, and move things around. On AmiPro there is also a Thesaurus, a spell-check and a grammar check, which I think improves my work.
>
> (Girl, Year 10.)

The value which computers create in work done for school were clearly perceived. As long as marks were awarded for presentation and lack of surface errors, then the use of a computer would enable you to score more highly than if one had not been used.

> ... they can get you marks for presentation, spelling, punctuation and sentence structure. If I do a draft and want to change it, it is quicker and easier than scribbling and making the paper messy, so you can read it.
>
> (Girl, Year 10.)

The cumulative effect of these programs on student work was to produce a document hegemony. A document is qualitatively and quantitatively different from an essay. A document will contain sections with appropriate titles, charts, tables and clip art, page numbers and possibly footnotes. Students who used word processing programs were enabled to produce such documents, especially if they used templates or wizards. Because they were able to produce such artefacts, the expectation developed that all work should be reproduced in such a way. The expectation initially took root among the students, where it became the norm - the accepted and expected way of working. This in turn became the expectation of their teachers, most of whom were themselves unable to produce such documents. (This is illustrated in Chapter 5: 'What teachers think about IT.')

The documents were paginated, used a range of text formatting styles (often based on document templates), incorporated checking systems such as spelling, Thesaurus and grammar and produced a high-quality print-out. Reference sources from CD-ROM were often pasted into such documents at will.

> I have a CD-ROM at home and find it very useful when doing projects ... (it) could result in getting better marks as you have more info on the topic.
>
> (Girl, Year 9.)

In other words, using information that was not available at school, and which, by its very nature was up-to-date, generated added value. The quantity of work produced in this way is likely to increase as students move from Key Stage 3 to 4 and GCSE. For the 94-96 GCSE cohort at the school the average was 30 substantial pieces of coursework during five terms.

Students clearly perceived the impact of a personal computer on productivity.

> The amount of time spent on homework is still the same but when on computer you end up doing more detailed work and more of it too.
>
> (Boy, Year 10.)

> I find it a lot quicker to write up on a computer, and I find it much easier to write as it all just flows out.
>
> (Girl, Year 10.)

Access to programs which would facilitate the production process became a priority during this period.

> ... if you don't have a computer and your handwriting is not too good then you could lose marks for being untidy...
>
> (Boy, Year 9.)

> It won't get you extra marks for content, you may get some for presentation. It may be possible, though, to pick up extra marks if you use a special program like Encarta 95 ... an easily operated, vast encyclopedia with many facts and lots of information. At home it will help improve research skills and speed up the time doing it, so you can get more written content in your work.
>
> (Boy, Year 10.)

The student recognises the importance of presentation, and although he distances himself from saying directly that he will earn more marks for it, he is aware that the medium and the message are closely intertwined.

> ... I do find that I do get better marks when I use a computer for my work but I think this is because when doing work on the computer you think about what you're doing more.
>
> (Girl, Year 10.)

The approach of students to schoolwork, coursework and assignments is linked to the information technology resources available to them, whether at home or at school.

> ... it is easy to change things, and move things around ... there is also a Thesaurus, a spell-check and a grammar check, which I think improves my work.
>
> (Girl, Year 10.)

A consequence of this is that the amount of time which is spent using computers for work, and the range and volume of the tasks undertaken, is often far greater than that of their teachers. Mention has already been made of the average of thirty documents that students produce in five terms of GCSE coursework.

> I think that no matter what teachers say about you not getting any extra marks for the work being printed, a well-presented piece of typed work with (obviously) no crossings-out and no spelling mistakes can make a teacher go "Wow!" as soon as they see it.
>
> (Boy, Year 10.)

Student computer use

Students see computers as an integral part of their lives: all of the students in the school surveys (1995; 1996; 1997) who listed more than one use of a machine cited schoolwork as the primary use, with games as a method of relaxation.

Students saw the main use of computers for work as word-processing. Correct spelling, legibility of text and good presentation were consistently cited as reasons for using a computer. Comments previously cited illustrate this (52% of users Year 7; 42% of users Year 10; 32% of users Year 12).

The production of documents, rather than simple pages of text, is stated as becoming more important through Year 9 into Year 10. The ability to incorporate graphs, tables and clip art into a document was seen in transactional terms: the better produced the document, the higher the grade it was likely to earn (57 % of users).

Student reference to, and use of, spreadsheets was therefore seen as a means to an end - charts and tables - which were to be incorporated into documents.   The use of databases, on the other hand, was restricted to specific subject applications.   These were Mathematics (Years 7-9) or Business Studies and Economics (Years 10-11).   Students rarely perceived databases as a way of organizing information to achieve their own ends. Only from Year 12 onwards were databases seen as a way of organizing and manipulating data.

Most students at this time viewed computers as a tool for information access and retrieval through use of CD-ROM and Multimedia. A consistent reason for using computers was given as '...learning about things...', but few linked the structure and content of the CD-ROM with databases. (This resulted in inefficient or inappropriate CD-ROM searches: '...there isn't anything about...' or, even worse, hundreds of 'hits' in which a single word had been identified.   Search routines needed to be taught, rather than simply acquired.   As the Internet became the default information source this problem became even more acute.)

The concept of 'learning about things' is explored later in the study, in students' concepts of Mind.

The 58% overall response in the survey of students using a computer for work suggested that students saw it as a tool.   The application of the computer to work increased in frequency as the students moved through school.

(The March 1999 survey showed 81% of students in the school with a computer at home and using it for work: Year 7: 77%; Year 8: 80%; Year 9: 78%; Year 10: 84%; Year 11: 84%; Years 12/13: 85%.)

Gratifications: why students say they use computers

When the survey was initiated one purpose was to identify the reasons students gave for using computers.   It was decided to use a 'Uses and Gratifications' methodology.   (A more detailed explanation for this choice can be found in Chapter 2.)   The students were asked to complete a form with two prompts: 'I use computers for ... because...' for both school and home use.   The data for the analysis of Gratifications was drawn from the responses to the prompt 'because...', which were then collated into sets.   Four separate sets of responses emerged.

Table 4.8: Gratifications: responses by type

Category	Diversion	Relationship	Personal Identity			Surveillance
			(a) Personal reference	(b) Reality exploration	(c) Value reinforcement	
Female	51%	1%	16%	4%	96%	16%
Male	69%	1%	28%	5%	97%	18%
Total	60%	1%	22%	4%	96%	17%

The research literature on young people and computer use does not provide a taxonomy for classifying these responses. A framework therefore had to be constructed to enable such a classification. Whilst the existing literature on computer uses and young people (Underwood and Underwood, 1990) at the time the investigation began had no model, one could be found within Media Studies. Audience research into television use by young people had developed a functionalist perspective based on a 'Uses and Gratifications' model. (McQuail, 1969; 1981; 1987). The framework of what people use television for, and their reasons for so doing, suggested that a similar approach could be applied to another medium. A Taxonomy of Computer Uses was devised.

Information Technology and its uses: media, audience and the escapist thesis

One approach to the use of Information Technology by young people treats the subject as an extension of the entertainment media. The focus is on the recreational aspects of computer use: young consumers purchase interactive media and games, and the users are therefore regarded as an audience. Their uses of IT media are seen from the same perspective as their uses of other media. The dominant interpretation of media uses by young people is that of entertainment, particularly 'escapist' entertainment. Such interpretations have developed into moral panics focused around such issues as racism, sexism and violence in computer games, VDUs as a vector for epilepsy and global computer pornography delivered via the Internet. Indeed, there is a Center for Online Addiction to cater for misuses of ICT (www.netaddiction.com (1998)).

Whether or not entertainment and 'escape' can be seen as 'good' depends on the ideological position of the writer. The concept of entertainment as escape essentially derives from a nineteenth-century view of popular culture, which is seen as oppositional to 'high' culture. This was the perspective which informed the work of media researchers such as Lowenthal (1950) and Schramm, Lyle and Parker (1961). Others (Horton and Wohl) saw media use as a social alternative, or as 'parasocial interaction', in which gratifications sought could include emotional release, stimulus or vicarious compensations. Some identified the 'mythic' function of modern entertainment (Morin, 1960).

Much of the evidence for these theses is based on data that apparently indicates that heavy use of media is associated with personal/social deprivation; media analysis that proves there is persistent reality distortion and the popularity of material that is considered to be without intrinsic merit. The 'escape' thesis is regarded as proven by the final fact the use of mass media is a matter of free personal choice. These perspectives and assumptions have been transferred to an analysis of the interaction between young people (predominantly male) and computers.

Some early audience studies into television use focused on the concept of the viewer as consumer, in that individuals in a democracy (or free market) had freedom of consumer choice. In 'TV as a common culture', (Westley and MacLean, 1957), had treated mass media provision and consumer selections as a reflection of the general needs of the social system to orient itself to its environment. Rosengren and Windahl (1972) established a number of correlations between mass media consumption and direct interpersonal interaction, and found that the fewer the opportunities for interaction, the higher the reliance on mass media content. This interpretation has developed and refined itself in relation to computer use, whilst at the same time establishing a dichotomous interpretation of its effects. When the effects can be seen to reduce commuting and develop the use of telecottages, they are good; when the effects are seen to encourage young people to spend hours in front of a VDU, they are bad.

Uses and gratifications

The relationship between media and its audiences can be considered from another perspective. The 'Uses and Gratifications' approach, at its most simplistic, asks: who uses which media; under what circumstances and for what reasons. 'Uses and Gratifications' has its origins in opposition to deterministic assumptions about media effects; it was termed 'the rediscovery of people' (Katz and Lazarsfeld, 1955). There was in addition an understandable desire to break out of the debate over mass media taste, in which the elitist position would hold that, since bad art drives out good, mass media must, per se, be Bad. 'Uses and Gratifications' could be seen as a Functionalist approach to the study of media, where the media can be considered as a part of the individual's immediate environment (Fearing, 1947).

The first phase of 'Uses and Gratifications' theories, its 'classical' period, used a description of audience sub-group orientations to selected media content to establish the uses to which it was put: radio, (Herzog, 1944; Suchman, 1942); newspapers, (Berelson, 1949). The second phase can be termed its 'modern' period, in which attempts were made to use gratifications data to provide explanations of the communication process (Katz et al., 1975).

Children and computer use

The conceptual framework of the mass media 'Uses and Gratifications', and in particular its application to the young television viewer, provides a tool through which the use of computers by young people may be analysed. Three studies provide particularly pertinent insights.

Himmelweit, Oppenheim and Vince

Himmelweit's Theory of Displacement, in the comprehensive study 'Television and the Child' (1958), suggests that TV viewing displaces activities which are functionally similar. The study was an extremely detailed analysis of the interaction between children and television in the United Kingdom. The Displacement Theory was perhaps their most significant finding, in that it implicitly identified reasons for viewing. The study was concerned to investigate the effects that television had on children's lives. It examined what children did with television and the uses to which they put it.

Greenberg

The child audience study in London, (Greenberg, 1972) constructed a typology of uses. Children were asked about the gratifications they obtained from TV viewing by completing the sentence 'I watch TV because ...'. The answers were grouped under eight headings, with sub-groups: Relaxation; Companionship; Learning about things; Habit; To pass time; Learning about myself; Arousal and To forget.

McQuail et al.

The 1972 study of television audiences in Leeds and its 1975 modification (McQuail and Gurevitch) defined a range of uses to which television was put by its audiences. Greenberg's typology was updated and synthesized by McQuail, whose 1987 categories were grouped under the headings of Information, Personal Identity, Social Integration and Entertainment. This typology forms perhaps the most definitive analysis of the uses to which television is put, and the reasons people give for using it. One conclusion that was drawn from this was that the emphasis in any study must therefore be on the processes through which the content is used. This reinforced the findings of Cullingford (1984).

User taxonomies

From the findings of the various studies McQuail constructed a number of taxonomies. The first is one of media-person interactions, and provides the most effective tool for examining computer use by young people.

Diversion
        a) Escape from constraints of routine;
        b) Escape from burdens of problems;
        c) Emotional release;
Personal relationships
        a) Companionship;
        b) Social utility; TV is used as a 'coin of exchange' - a common area of experience for talk.
Personal identity
        a) Personal reference;
        b) Reality exploration;
        c) Value reinforcement;
Surveillance
        Material for information and opinions about events in the wider world.

McQuail's observation on this typology is that researchers should expect to encounter changes in it for three main reasons. First, as a result of changes in audience experience and perception; second, as a result of changes in communication patterns (and technology); and finally, as a result of changes in social patterns. These comments were made about television and its audience. The speed of technological change, the status of computers as a consumer good with peripherals priced to stimulate the demand of a young market and the promotion of IT through the education process are factors that make this typology even more susceptible to change.

Computer use gratifications

The four main categories of gratification identified by McQuail for people's use of television provide immediate parallels with young people's use of computers. The questionnaire was designed to examine who used which type of computer; under what circumstances and for what reasons. The focus throughout was on the processes through which computers were used by young people.

The first set of categories are Diversion. The responses cited entertainment, escape from boredom, excitement, a break from work and fun. What was significant in this grouping, however, was the number of students for whom doing work on the computer constituted 'fun'.

The second set dealt with the use of computers for establishing, developing or maintaining social relationships: Integration.

The third set, Personal Identity, constituted the greatest number of responses and consisted of three subsets: awareness and knowledge of computer applications; the transfer of skills and concepts to develop work; the uses to which hardware, software and peripherals could be, and were, put.

The final set of responses, Surveillance, dealt with the use of computers for extending skills and knowledge - finding out about things. Frequent reference was made to the use of CD-ROMS and other information-based software. Later surveys identified Internet use.

Student comments have been taken from response sheets.

1. Diversion (Entertainment)

a) Escape from constraints of routine:
    "I play games when I need a break from my work/other things...";
b) Escape from burdens of problems:
    "If I can't do my work I play a game to take my Mind off things...";
c) Emotional release:
    "I play when I'm bored, or when I need to relax"...;

2. Personal relationships (Integration)

a) Companionship: working with a friend on an assignment; playing games;
b) social utility: games (and their strategies) are used as a 'coin of exchange' - a common area of experience for talk;
c) using the computer to produce work for the family.

3. Personal identity

a) Personal reference: the development of computer skills and a knowledge base: students were concerned to demonstrate their knowledge of their computers and what they could do.   The emphasis was on systems and programs that could be identified as 'real', rather than those of school.
    "   on my PC we have AmiPro, for a word-processing package and Lotus 1-2-3 as a spreadsheet program ...";
b) Reality exploration: understanding how and why to undertake tasks on the computer:
    "... it is easy to change things, and move things around ... there is also a Thesaurus, a spell-check and a grammar check, which I think improves my work."
    The student recognises the importance of mastery, of being in control of the computer.
c) Value reinforcement: the perceived correlation between computer-produced work and better grades:
    " ... I do find that I do get better marks when I use a computer for my work but I think this is because when doing work on the computer you think about what you're doing more."
    This was a particularly strong response.   A number of students at Y10 and 11 commented that IT skills were now a prerequisite for most jobs:
    "...Computers are expensive but if you didn't have one you probably would be degraded because of it in later life ..."

4. Surveillance (Information)

This is interpreted as providing the student with material for information and opinions about events in the wider world. It represents finding out independently, of being able to access knowledge as and when the student wants. The use of Careers databases in and CD-ROM in the School

Library, Multimedia at home and the Internet were all cited by a range of students as a way of being able to find out about all the topics which might be of interest.

" ... Computers with reference software, such as "Encarta" (an interactive multi-media CD-ROM encyclopedia) are great for research." "...Encarta 95 ... an easily operated, vast encyclopedia with many facts and lots of information. At home it will help improve research skills and speed up the time doing it, so you can get more written content in your work..."

Table 4.9: Gratifications: a summary of findings

Diversion	Y7	Y8	Y9	Y10	Y11	Y12
Female	76%	71%	72%	28%	19%	19%
Male	86%	85%	97%	64%	44%	36%
Total	81%	78%	84%	49%	32%	29%

Integration	Y7	Y8	Y9	Y10	Y11	Y12
Female	4%	1%	1%	0%	0%	0%
Male	1%	2%	0%	0%	1%	1%
Total	3%	1%	1%	0%	0%	1%

Identity	Y7	Y8	Y9	Y10	Y11	Y12
Female	99%	91%	97%	96%	95%	97%
Male	97%	94%	100%	100%	100%	97%
Total	98%	93%	98%	98%	98%	91%

Information	Y7	Y8	Y9	Y10	Y11	Y12
Female	3%	16%	16%	27%	12%	33%
Male	6%	13%	35%	22%	12%	25%
Total	5%	14%	25%	24%	12%	29%

Gratifications analysis

Two sets of gratification dominate the responses: from the Diversion category, Diversion and Pleasure, and from the Identity category, value reinforcement.

Table 4.10: Diversion and pleasure

	Y7	Y8	Y9	Y10	Y11	Y12
Female	76%	71%	72%	28%	19%	19%
Male	86%	85%	97%	64%	44%	36%
Total	81%	78%	84%	49%	32%	29%

The use of computers as an entertainment tool peaks at Year 9 for boys: for girls there is a slight downward trend from Year 7 through Year 9. Thereafter there is a sharp downturn. Although Entertainment still constitutes a significant gratification, the imperatives of GCSE coursework re-focus computer use.   Despite this, a number of students at Years 10 and 11 use the gratification 'fun' to describe coursework using computers: "It's more fun on the computer ...".

Figure 4.4: Computer gratifications: diversion and pleasure

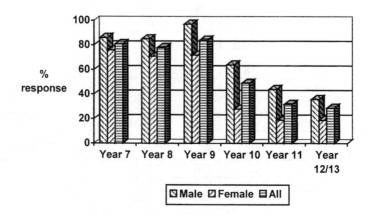

Table 4.11: Personal relationships (integration)

Integration	Y7	Y8	Y9	Y10	Y11	Y12
Female	4%	1%	1%	0	0	0
Male	1%	2%	0	0	1%	1%
Total	3%	1%	1%	0	0	1%

The percentage response for this section was the lowest of all of the gratifications cited by students. Despite the apparent low response, however, personal observation would suggest that computers and their applications are a focus of conversation and thus facilitate relationships. Conversations range from ways in which to manipulate data for assignments, to ways in which to progress through computer games. A significant point is the way in which conversation focuses on sets of abstract procedures: data handling and manipulation or shared imaginative access to games world (McShane, 1991). The final survey, in 1999, took place before the explosion of email use among young people, based on free, web-based email services.

Personal identity

Table 4.12: Personal reference: the development of computer skills

	Y7	Y8	Y9	Y10	Y11	Y12
Female	7%	8%	23%	43%	52%	31%
Male	6%	3%	22%	39%	16%	17%
Total	6%	6%	23%	42%	34%	25%

These responses, as a percentage of the total number of responses, show a sharp upward trend from Year 8 through Year 10, with only slight variation for Gender, would suggest that the ubiquity of PCs with a Windows operating system has established a software hegemony in the Minds of the students. Their concept of what constitutes a computer, its operating system and software are all predicated on Microsoft software and PC architecture. What is clear, however, is that many students have a detailed knowledge of programs and the operating systems which they can customise to their advantage. This reaches its peak for Year 11 males, who are at the stage where they feel that they can at least establish mastery over one aspect of their lives.

Figure 4.5: Personal reference: the development of computer skills

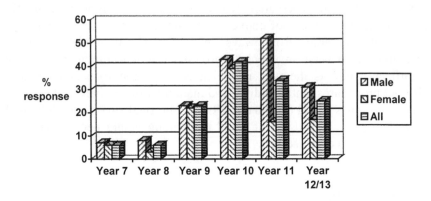

Table 4.13: Reality exploration: understanding how and why to undertake tasks on the computer

	Y7	Y8	Y9	Y10	Y11	Y12
Female	3%	4%	3%	9%	2%	2%
Male	5%	3%	4%	9%	5%	0%
Total	4%	4%	4%	9%	4%	1%

Year 10, with 9% citations for knowing how and why to undertake tasks on the computer, represents the peak of responses. One explanation for such low responses throughout the age and gender range could be that the processes and concepts are internalised, so for many students this gratification represents an integral part of computer use. Such students could be said to be in transition from embedded to disembedded thinking, in that they are able to transfer learned patterns of behaviour to the creation of new objects. They are demonstrating competence, freed from their old limitations (Donaldson, 1987). Disembodied thought involves the manipulation of symbols: however, far from being abstract, the symbols young users manipulate on their computers have tangible links to the concrete and the artefacts that they create. Another reason may be more fundamental, in that, whilst many students have an implicit understanding of how and why they do things, they are unable to explain this (Cf. Vygotsky, 1962). This has implications for the demands placed on students (and teachers) by the National Curriculum.

Figure 4.6: Reality exploration: the understanding of computer tasks

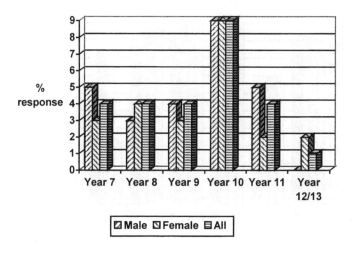

Table 4.14: Personal identity: value reinforcement

(The perceived correlation between computer-produced work and better grades.)

	Y7	Y8	Y9	Y10	Y11	Y12
Female	99%	91%	97%	96%	95%	97%
Male	97%	94%	100%	100%	100%	87%
Total	98%	93%	98%	98%	98%	91%

This was the strongest and most consistent gratification cited by students. The perception that using a computer to produce coursework resulted in higher grades is a recurring theme in students' comments. The survey of teacher perceptions and uses of Information Technology in the following section would appear to confirm student perceptions.

Figure 4.7: Personal identity: computer use and value reinforcement

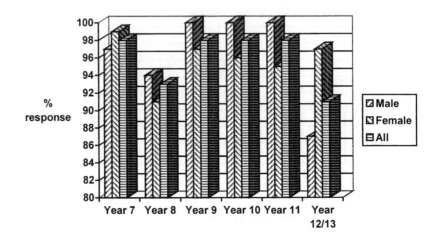

Table 4.15: Surveillance

(Material for information and opinions about the wider world.)

	Y7	Y8	Y9	Y10	Y11	Y12
Female	3%	16%	16%	27%	12%	33%
Male	6%	13%	35%	22%	12%	25%
Total	5%	14%	25%	24%	12%	29%

Whilst part of the reason for the number of responses in this category can be ascribed awareness of the Internet and Multimedia, or even access to these at home, it was the integration of CD-ROM and multimedia packages in into the Year and Departmental curriculum that had the most significant effect.   As part of Careers Education Year 9 students used databases such as JobFile Explorer: post-16 students used databases such as ECCTIS and PUSH.   This would explain the response peaks, in Years 9 and 12. Other groups used CD-ROM disks as information sources within the curriculum: The Times on CD-ROM, Encarta and other multimedia encyclopaedias, Interactive Shakespeare, and so on.

Figure 4.8: Surveillance: information about the wider world

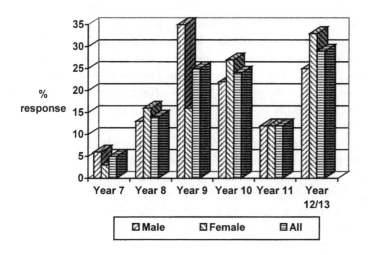

Two main conclusions can be drawn from these findings.

The first is that the responses form a close fit with the categories developed by McQuail for the gratifications cited by young people for television use. This four-part taxonomy would seem to be an appropriate framework for computer gratifications, both in the range of responses generated by young people and in the fact that, during the whole period of the survey, these responses were consistent.

The second conclusion is that the majority of the gratifications are extremely functional: they fall into the category of Personal Identity, and, in particular, the sub-set of value reinforcement. Students see computers as a tool for amplification, for the enhancement of their work. Earlier comments have indicated the centrality of ICT to the ways in which students see themselves as fitting into a learning community and the wider post-industrial world. Personal identity responses recognise this fact: the value reinforcement sub-set works both in the context of school work (see Appendix 1 and Appendix 2) and the wider world of employment.

Over time one would expect to see the percentage of responses for Surveillance increase, as more students use Internet, CD-ROM and Multimedia information sources. At the time of writing the factor that inhibits home use of the Internet is that of telephone costs. This is particularly apposite when telephone accounts are a frequent site of conflict between parents and their children.

The Relationships category, on the other hand, is one for which few students made explicit mention: at an implicit level, however, computer use, especially in school, generates a range of relationships as students work together (Somekh, 1986; Somekh and Davis, 1991; 1997; Underwood and Underwood, 1990). It may be that, although students regularly work in twos or threes at computers, this is not to be perceived as constituting a relationship. It is work. The same is true for interactions about computer games. As previously noted, these responses were made before the mass availability of email. At the time of the survey only those with an internet service provider had access to email.

Discussions are often seen as information exchange, rather than the basis for inter-personal discourse. One feature of studies of television gratifications, however, is that, whilst most respondents cite 'entertainment' as the main reason for viewing, many go on to discuss the value of television as a 'coin of exchange' (Morley, 1986) in social situations. This is an aspect which applies to discourse about the use of computer games as well as ways in which to use specific applications to produce work for school.

Reality exploration is the most problematic sub-set of the Personal Identity category. One reason for this may well be the constant focus on outcomes, rather than processes, that has been at the heart of the school IT RoA programme. Another may well be that this is, in fact, how people view computers and their uses: tools of the mind and tools of the hand. (Bruner, 1966; cf. University of Sussex study of teleworkers; staff responses to the computer use survey.) Computers as objects are real. The processes which are undertaken on them are virtual. Outcomes produced by computers as a result of virtual processes are real. This modality judgement on the part of the majority of students in the survey may well explain why the response rate for reality exploration was so low (1 - 9%). The high of 9% was recorded in Year 10, when there is a significant learning curve associated with the use of computers for examination coursework.

Whatever the reason may be, there is a need to make much more explicit the concepts of data handling. The observations of Vygotsky, that learners are able to undertake operations without necessarily being able to fully explain the processes underlying them, would seem to suggest that a focus on the language involved in the processes and concepts should be a central part of the teaching process. Study of student conversations relating to computers (mentioned earlier) may provide a way forward (Whorf, 1956).

The development of a hegemony: PCs and student use

The first survey at BSCS, during the academic year 1994-95, sought to identify those students who used a computer at home. Students identified the type of machine to which they had access, and the uses to which it was put. Table 16 shows those who said that they had a computer which they could use for work, as opposed to those which could only be used for games playing. During this survey many of the students identified difficulties they had with computers such as Amiga and Atari, which they tried to use for work but which were more suited for games-playing. A consistent comment from students was that they wished that they had a PC, which they saw as a 'real' computer.

Table 4.16: 1995 survey

Total number of respondents with a computer at home (n=1132).

All types: work and games	PC ownership
733	466
(58%)	(35%)

Survey comparisons: observations

The increasing facility of young people to utilize computing resources in their work suggested that they had internalized the routines and skills required by the software which they employed. Comments made by students in Years 9 and 10 obtained during the second survey, which asked them whether they thought it worthwhile to obtain a computer for schoolwork (quoted in earlier sections), bear this out.

The ways in which students used computers reflected their facility. Comments which students made through every survey substantiated this. One example was that

> ... I do find that I do get better marks ... you think about what you're doing more.
>
> (Girl, Year 10.)

This student perceived the enhanced marks as a consequence of thinking more: the computer enabled her to do that. It was not simply a cynical reflex that equated neat word processing with a higher mark. Each survey indicated an increasing number of students using their home computers for work, and spending more time on their work. They enjoyed it, often referring to it as 'fun'. It generated a sense of pride and ownership.

The resources that they deployed shaped the ways in which they worked.

> ... it is easy to change and move things ... there is also a Thesaurus, a spell-check and a grammar check.
>
> (Girl, Year 10.)

Work was therefore subject to constant revision and improvement. The time that the students spent working on computers increased with the resources available to them.

Teacher uses

Teachers spent far less of their working day using computers than students. A similar survey to that of the students indicated that such use as took place primarily involved the production of worksheets for students (74% of respondents cited 'typing' - word-processing as their main use) or administration: entering orders on the school SIMS terminal (School Information Management System), or student data for departmental records. This involved the production of class and set lists, rank order lists and other administrative tasks. Teachers undertook these tasks on school PCs or Archimedes machines, or on machines at home. No year team, department or member of staff indicated that data from SIMS was used for this task, or that SIMS itself was used. SIMS was regarded as an electronic order-generating machine. The reality is that it can be used for a wide range of data-handling and data processing tasks, which can then be integrated with other programs.

Teachers also used equipment at home far less than did students. Whilst 43% of staff respondents had access to a PC at home, only 57% of this total stated that they used the PC for word-processing - the most frequently cited activity. Teachers consistently used the word 'typing' to describe this.

In other words, fewer than 25% of the school staff used a computer at home - even though 43% of the staff had access to one.

The primary use of their computers was for word-processing: the production of worksheets, correspondence, church newsletters or recipes.

The survey was repeated in late spring 1996 to determine whether the same increase in PC ownership and access had occurred as with students during the same period. Ownership and access appeared to have increased to 52% of staff respondents.

However, only 60% of the teaching staff completed the return. When the non-return of the questionnaire was followed up with individuals the response could be generalised as lack of interest in, and knowledge of, computers. If the staff total was used as a base, therefore, and we assumed that teachers who failed to complete a return neither used information technology in school nor owned a computer, an even more negative picture emerged.

Table 4.17: Computer use at school and home: teacher response, 1996

Staff	n=111	W/P	S/S	D/B	CD-ROM	CAL	CAD	Control	Internet	Video-conferencing
School use	40% (44)	40% (44)	11% (12)	18% (20)	7% (8)	29% (32)	6% (7)	2% (2)	4% (4)	4% (4)
Home use	32% (35)	32% (35)	11% (12)	11% (12)	9% (10)			1% (1)	4% (4)	

(Key: W/P = word processing; S/S = spreadsheets; D/B = database; CAL = Computer Assisted Learning; CAD = Computer Aided Design; Control = Control Technology.)
Numbers in brackets refer to the numbers of teachers using particular applications.

This would suggest that the staff as a whole may not have internalized the skills and concepts implicit in the application of computers to work in the same way as had students. It would support current government assumptions on the need for in-service education to improve teachers' computer competence – the New Opportunities Fund.

This disjunction has had serious implications for teachers.

> Once you have finished and the teacher asks you to add or do it again you can say "OK" without a face.
>
> (Boy, Year 9.)

Access to a computer enables instant and easy revisions. Students are able to focus on changes to the content, rather than on re-writing a complete piece of work.

Conclusions

In 1988, one Year 10 student at Boston Spa Comprehensive School regularly produced documents with embedded charts and tables. Other students were able to wordprocess text and generate accompanying charts and tables. The majority of students had to hand-produce assignments: their expectations were framed by the skills and time available to them, and their work shaped accordingly.

The comments from Year 9 and Year 10 students during the research undertaken during the summer term of 1995 show that an overwhelming majority of students saw the boundary of their possibilities at a different level. For them, the technology available to them represented their limit. Those students who did not have access to these facilities at home, or who did not use them at school, were still aware of what was possible. Their peers provided compelling evidence of what could be done. The aphorism 'The Medium Is The Message' (McLuhan, 1964) had altered for our students. Not only did the medium determine the way in which the message was read, but it also determined the way it was produced - and, inevitably, the content.

The accelerating ownership levels of personal computers among school students had been accompanied by an increase in use, both in terms of the time spent using machines, and the range of tasks for which they are used. Students have internalized information technology concepts which may well be different from those of their teachers. Students see the product as the integration of a number of computer facilities through their computer skills. They use and synthesize information, rather than selecting and filtering it. The availability of Internet and CD-ROM information sources presents a range of informational possibilities: far greater than those a student could access in a conventional school library, or from domestic reference books. Students no longer rephrase one or two text sources for their assignments: they select from a range of them and assemble a collage. They epitomize what has been described as the post-modern condition (Baudrillard, 1987), in which no text or source is privileged over another.

Curriculum applications of Information Technology, especially those required by the Statutory Orders of the National Curriculum, sit unhappily with these practices. Much current pedagogy seeks to identify opportunities to integrate Information Technology applications with specific sections of subject curricula. On the other hand, students who use their computers for as much of their work as possible integrate their subjects with the appropriate applications of their computers and their skills. This disjunction is explored in a later section.

Students concern themselves with the final product, and the way in which their computing resources can be used to shape that. The ways in which the text is generated will determine the text itself. Similarly, the range of charts which can be produced from a set of data will stimulate critical responses to the data itself. When students can, with a minimum of effort, generate and print one chart after another they are able to discern patterns and trends, rather than having to determine what the pattern or trend was, and then produce an accompanying chart.

Reflections

Throughout this research I was aware of the disjunction between the processes and attitudes that students brought to the work which they undertook on computers at home, and that which they did at school. Recurrent responses in the 'because' section of the school survey were 'because it's in the National Curriculum'; 'because we have to'; 'it's part of Maths'; 'the teacher makes us'. Home was seen as the site of production, the place where serious work could be done, and where the student was able to control the working environment, particularly with the computer.

This raised a number of issues for teachers. One was a matter of control. How did the teacher cope when a significant number of the class had made the decision to work at home? Were students right when they said that work produced on the computer earned more marks? How could teachers redress the balance for those who did not have access to a computer at home?

The OFSTED inspections of 1993 – 1997 found that IT capability was poor in 40% of schools inspected, with a lack of coherent development, particularly at key Stage 4 (Years 10 and 11).

With each survey I undertook the issues became more clear-cut. There was a significant difference between what students were using their computers for at home and what they were using them for at school. As teachers we found ourselves struggling to link the potential of home and school and embed it into the curriculum.

Surprises

As the percentage of students with access to a home computer increased the initial gender disparity, in which more males than females had access to a computer, reduced.   As the distinction between a computer which could only be used for playing games and one which could be used for both work and games disappeared, so the number of girls with a computer which they used for work increased.   In part this was due to the marketing of multimedia PCs, with CD-ROM reference tools, as a consumer good from Christmas 1996 onwards.   In part it was also due to the fall in the price of printers, particularly colour printers.   PCs were now seen as creative, rather than technical, tools.

For the final survey there was no significant gender difference in use and ownership of personal computers.

The first survey had indicated that a significant number of students had access to a personal computer at home and were using it for work.   It also demonstrated that there was a perception at a 'real' computer was a PC running Windows-based software similar to those found in most office. This was contrasted with many of the computers students encountered in an educational environment, which were seen as in the control of their teachers and part of the school curriculum.   As the number of students using a home PC increased so did perceptions as to what constituted a 'real' computer and how it should be used.   Increasingly these perceptions were at variance with the expectations and expertise of their teachers.

These disparities are explored in Chapter 5.

5 What teachers think about ICT

Background

The first survey had shown a significant number of students using a computer at home. This number increased with every survey, so that by the 1999 survey ownership ranged from 77% in Year 7 to 85% in Year 12/13. 81% of the school had a PC at home that they used for work, information and leisure.

Surveys into student computer use had been extended to teaching staff on each occasion. Teacher use of computers had consistently been below that of students, both in terms of the range of applications and the amount of time spent using computers. Factors leading to this have been identified as the problems of integrating IT activities into the prescriptions of the National Curriculum and difficulties in managing the learning environment of a computer-resourced classroom. The range of computer systems cited by teachers were predominantly those to be found in schools (see Table 18). When ownership of computers was examined, many teachers commented on the high cost of PCs as a proportion of taxed income. There was also an unwillingness on the part of some teachers to purchase something that would only lead to them producing more work in their own time. Despite these reservations most teachers expressed the view that there were benefits for students using them.

It was decided to extend the survey beyond the staff at Boston Spa Comprehensive School to identify teacher ownership of and attitudes towards computers and their use for schoolwork.

Methodology

During the academic year 1996/7 a sample of teachers in the Leeds L.E.A. was surveyed to identify their perception of the impact of computers on students' work. The survey was carried out at Boston Spa Comprehensive

School, (BSCS) City Comprehensive School (CCS) and an L.E.A. professional development centre (PDC).

The scope of, and background to, the sample is as follows. Number of respondents: BSCS=61; CCS=24; PDC=31. Teachers were asked whether they had a home computer and, if so, what type it was and the purpose for which it was used.

Table 5.1: 1996-97 Teachers and computers: overall ownership patterns

PC	Acorn	BBC	Mac	Amiga	Atari	Psion
58%	20%	1.7%	3.4%	0.9%	0.9%	0.9%

Figure 5.1: 1996-97 Teachers and computers: ownership by type

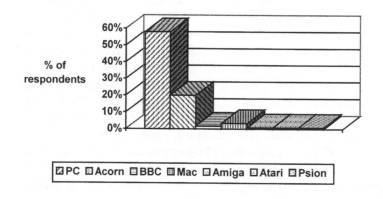

Although, by 1997, a PC running a Windows operating system had become the de facto standard for personal computing, it is significant than 20% of teachers owned and used an Acorn computer: either an Archimedes, or the older BBC Acorn. Many schools within Leeds LEA were still equipped with Acorn Archimedes, and their forerunners. Very few schools, on the other hand, used Apple Macintosh computers, compared with art colleges.

Responses to the survey

1. *What do you feel has been the main impact of computers on students' work?*

Table 5.2: Impact of computers on student work

Impact	All (n=116)
Presentation	37%
Motivation	17%
CD-ROM Research	10%
Word-processing	4%
Project work - documents	3%
Computer Literacy	1.7%
Control Technology	1.7%
Integration of syllabus topics	1.7%
Understanding of concepts	1.7%
Computer as an extra tool	0.86%
Drafting to improve content	0.86%
Statistical modelling	0.86%
Variety of teaching styles	0.86%

Whilst some teachers failed to respond to this question, others cited more than one area in which they felt computer use had benefited student work. Teachers across all subject disciplines noted the effect of computers on the presentation of student work: more specific comments tended to be related to the curricular area for which the teacher had responsibility. This also applies to responses to Question 3. (Question 5 examines negative effects of computers on student work.)

2. *Do you feel the quality of the work has been improved by the use of computers?*

   Yes = 80%   No = 16%   No response = 4%

3. *What aspects of students' work has been improved by the use of computers? (Similar comments apply to responses for this section as for Question 1.)*

Table 5.3: Aspects of student work improved by computer use

Aspect	All (n=116)
Legibility	66%
Organisation of work	56%
Spelling	41%
Integration of text, tables and charts	41%
Grammatical structures	10%
Design graphics	2.5%
Increased problem-solving skills and statistical application	2.5%
Application to detail	1.7%
Increased output	1.7%
Detailed research	1.7%
Examination revision	0.86%
Enhanced self-esteem	0.86%
Enhanced conceptualisation	0.86%
Use of evidence	0.86%

The teachers' perceptions, therefore, were focused on presentation of the work which students generate, and the ways in which its elements are integrated. The predominance of word-processing in computer uses cited by staff respondents (71%) would correlate with this. If word-processing is the application most familiar to teachers, then these are the effects that will be most readily apparent when student work is assessed. The illocutionary message is that word-processed work, which is legible and well-organised will be rewarded more highly than hand-written work.

Teachers were asked whether they could quantify the improvement in terms of marks (Question 4).

Table 5.4: Percentage improvement

Improvement	0-15%	16-25%	26-50%	50%+
ALL	21% (23)	16% (19)	4% (5)	2.6 (3)

Table 5.5: Age of students affected

KS3	KS4	16+
53% (61)	65% (75)	35% (41)

43.6% of teachers, therefore, felt that the use of computers improved work by up to 15%, and the student cohort most affected was Key Stage 4 – those taking GCSE. Almost 23% felt that work was improved by up to 25%.

5. *Do you feel that the use of computers has had a negative effect on students' work?*

Table 5.6: Negative effects

YES	NO	No response
15% (17)	78% (91)	7%

Some 7% of teachers (8) identified the problem of 'Computer as scapegoat', in that students were able to use the computer as a reason for failing to submit work to deadlines. The limitations imposed by inadequate word-processing skills were also seen as a problem, together with an apparent lack of sequencing of work by some students. The use of inappropriate charts in documents was also seen as one of the negative affects produced by computers on students' work, where the focus was often on presentation, rather than content. One teacher commented that computers did not "…help…handwriting skills. Poor handwriting is not improved."

The significance of these comments lies more in what they reveal about the level of teacher intervention in students' work: teachers see themselves as judges of a finished product that is a reflection of a student's skills and abilities. What is required is dialogue between teacher and student during the process, rather than final comment on the finished product.

Among other negative factors identified were the transfer of work away from school for those who had a home PC, and the accompanying disadvantage of those without home facilities. Those who were reliant on school machines took a long time to complete a task: "…they spend a long time writing up assignments." There is still a tendency to view word-processing as a variant of typewriting, in that a student's work receives its final polish through the medium of the computer.

6.   *What are the benefits of encyclopedias and reference works on CD-ROM?*

Table 5.7: Benefits frequently cited

Positive Responses = 72% (84)
Improvement in information seeking
Up-to-date and relevant
Motivation
Ease of access
Ease of cross-referencing
Stimulating learning

7.   *Are there any drawbacks to these?*

Unselective use of material with no editing or integration 32% (37).
Also cited as drawbacks were theft of CD-ROMS and the 'play' factor: students would use CD-ROM encyclopedias and browse them for 'fun', rather than being 'serious' and using them 'for work'.

Teacher computer use

Teachers were asked to indicate uses to which they put computers at school, for personal and curricular outcomes. The curricular applications were then grouped in terms of the software used by teachers with students.

Table 5.8: Staff computer use as part of the curriculum

W/P	D/B	Charts	S/S	CAL	DTP	Internet	CD-ROM	CALL
62%	27%	22%	21%	13%	8.6%	7%	6%	3%
(72)	(31)	(26)	(24)	(15)	(10)	(8)	(7)	(4)

(Key: W/P = word processing; D/B = database; S/S = spreadsheets; DTP = desktop publishing; CAL = Computer Assisted Learning; CALL = Computer Assisted Language Learning.)

Figure 5.2: Teachers' use of computer applications

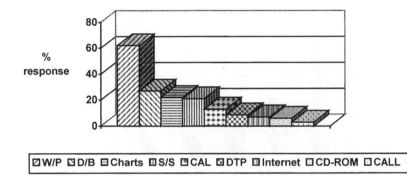

From this information, therefore, it can be seen that the majority of teachers focused on IT activities that produced short-term, measurable outcomes. These activities were also those undertaken at home, and ones with which the teachers themselves were most familiar.

Word processing was referred to as *'typing'* by most teacher respondents. This was the application used by most teachers on their home computers.

The focus on short-term, measurable outcomes carried across into the way in which teachers perceived the utility of what students did with computers.

When teachers were asked what impact they thought that computers had on students' work, their responses fell into three main categories. These can be grouped as transactional, cognitive or affective.

Not surprisingly, the most frequently cited set of responses fall into the category of transactional factors. This correlates with the most frequently cited curricular applications: word processing, databases, charts and spreadsheets.

**Figure 5.3: Impact on students' work: teacher perceptions (%
response)**

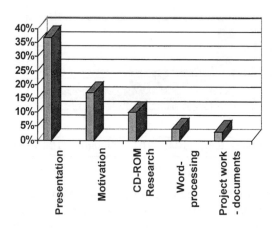

Presentation is the most visible factor when teachers assess student
work. Many students recognise this. (See student comments in Appendix
One: Coursework and Marks.)

**Figure 5.4: Aspects of work improved by computers: teacher
perceptions (% response)**

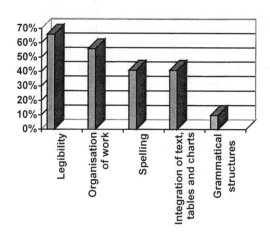

The four main aspects of work identified by teachers all relate to the surface of the work. When students are asked how they feel computers have improved their work a number of them refer to its more 'professional' look. (Further comments in Appendix One.)

What teachers think: an analysis

Table 5.9: Transactional factors

The main impact of computers on student work	n=116
Presentation	37%
Motivation	17%
CD-ROM Research	10%
Word-processing	4%
Project work - documents	3%

Aspect of work improved by student computer use	n=116
Legibility	66%
Organisation of work	56%
Spelling	41%
Integration of text, tables and charts	41%
Design graphics	2.5%

These figures confirm teacher perceptions of the effects of computer use on students' work.

Almost half of the teachers surveyed (43.6%) felt that work was improved by up to 15%.

Nearly one quarter (22.6%) felt that work was improved by up to 25%.

It is factors such as legibility, organisation of work, spelling, integration of text and tables and overall presentation that differentiate student work within mark schemes.

These outcomes are based on recognisable IT skills. Even teachers who do not use computers are able to identify these factors as contributing to the overall quality of a piece of work. In terms of a Uses and Gratifications taxonomy, most of the teachers are grounded at the level of **Personal Identity: Value Reinforcement**.

Implications

Teachers who do not teach their students how to use information technology to produce their work are effectively disadvantaging them. Those students will not score as highly when the work is assessed.

Schools that fail to provide skills input and computer access for students who do not have a machine at home are compounding the disadvantage.

Table 5.10: Impacts

The main impact of computers on student work	n=116	Aspect of work improved by student computer use	n=116
Computer literacy	1.7%	Grammatical structures	10%
Integration of syllabus topics	1.7%	Increased problem-solving skills and statistical application	2.5%
Understanding of concepts	1.7%		
Computer as an extra tool	0.86%		
Drafting to improve content	0.86%		
Stats modelling	0.86%		
Variety of teaching styles	0.86%		

Teachers in the survey had a limited perception of cognitive factors being improved by computer use. Eight items received mention: integration of syllabus topics; understanding of concepts; computer as a tool; drafting to improve content; statistical modelling, variety of teaching styles; grammatical structures and increased problem-solving skills.

An improvement in the use of grammatical structures was the most frequently cited benefit (10%), and it could be argued that the provision of grammar checking tools in word-processors were responsible for that benefit. There was no suggestion that this gain transferred itself into other writing environments.

Teachers' perception of the cognitive benefits of computer use, then, tend to be limited, subject specific and measured in terms of the curriculum element for which the teacher has responsibility. There is no overview of ways in which students use computers for work across the curriculum. There is no evaluation of overall cognitive benefits for students.

Table 5.11: Affective factors

Aspect of work improved by student computer use	(n=116)
Attention to detail	1.7%
Increased output and volume of work	1.7%
Detailed research	1.7%
Examination revision	0.86%
Enhanced self-esteem	0.86%
Enhanced conceptualisation	0.86%
Use of evidence	0.86%

Table 5.12: Transactional factors

The main impact of computers on student work	(n=116)
Motivation	17%
Integration of syllabus topics	1.7%
Understanding of concepts	1.7%
Drafting to improve content	0.86%

The chief significance of the teacher responses presented here is that motivation is the greatest impact cited in terms of affective factors (17% of teachers felt that computers improved motivation). This would suggest that the active element in working with computers is a motivator for those students who perceive the experience of being taught as essentially passive.

The contribution of computer use to the enhancement of affective factors was implicit within many of the comments made by teachers. The increased motivation of many students when they were able to work on computers was seen as crucial to the improvement of the work. In the same way in which students were able to invoke the computer as scapegoat, this same process enables their teachers to take a more impersonal, functional view of work. Changing text and reprinting work is easy: this encourages re-drafting of work and increases output.

Staff perceptions: a summary

Positive perceptions:
- 80%+ agreed that students work was improved by computer use. Teachers stressed legibility, presentation and organisation of work as the main areas of improvement.
- 43% of all teachers stated that work was improved by up to 15%.
- More than 70% of respondents cited use of CD-ROMS as beneficial.

Negative perceptions:
- The use of computers and CD-ROMs highlighted inadequate information handling skills. Whilst students were able to access and retrieve far more information by using CD-ROMs, there was limited integration of this information into the students' work.
- Students would often convert data into inappropriate charts.
- There were equal opportunities issues for those without a home PC.
- Reliance by students on computers for the production of work failed to develop other skills, such as handwriting. (This comment echoed many similar comments revealed in media research by those worried about the displacement effects of new technology: that radio would displace reading; that television would displace radio listening (Himmelweit, Oppenheim and Vince, 1958); that computers would …).

Teacher perspectives:
- 62% of the sample stated that they used computers in the curriculum for word-processing, although no frequency of use was cited. One survey of more than 3,400 teachers (Keele University, 1996) cited 70% as using the computers 'very infrequently'. Another found that four out of five teachers claimed that they were not familiar enough with computers to make full use of them in schools (Technology Colleges Trust, 1998). Although 43% of UK schools might have had computers connected to the Internet, only one third of these provided their pupils with Internet access. (British Educational Suppliers Association, 1998.)
- The teachers' main use of a computer was for word-processing (71%). This activity was, however, often cited as 'typing'.
- When teachers own a PC the site of production for work-related documents moves from school to home - as happens with many students.

What computers don't do

The concerns that teachers in the survey expressed about the use of computers in schools were not, in fact, about computers per se. The concerns were about other aspects of the curriculum that computer use highlighted. Teachers felt that computers failed to do a number of things.

They did not prevent students from evading responsibility: students were able to invoke technical failure, networking problems and lack of access as plausible reasons to avoid deadlines. Many students failed to make sure that they had adequate word-processing skills before they produced a piece of work, which meant that those teachers who themselves lacked those skills were unable to help them. The work itself took longer to produce, students often failed to save their work appropriately and had problems retrieving it at a later date.

Many students failed to use appropriate charts when converting data. Their lack of understanding meant that, whilst the software could easily convert data into a graphical format, the students were unable to choose the most appropriate format. Often the criteria for selecting a chart type were the colours and shapes on the screen.

Many teachers felt that computer use prevented many students from improving their handwriting skills, whilst at the same time they often spent too much time 'writing up' assignments.

The use of CD-ROMS posed problems for some teachers: students would unselectively print out passages from reference disks as their response to an assignment, whilst other students would steal the CD-ROMS.

Computer Assisted Learning (CAL) and Computer Assisted Language Learning programs (CALL) suffered when students used games-playing techniques and strategies with educational computer programs. These students saw the object of the exercise as 'winning' and achieving a high score, rather than using the program to reinforce learning. It may well be argued that despite this perception on the part of students, learning did take place, albeit at an implicit level. The significance of the reaction, however, is that it would appear to produce behavioural effects at variance with those expected in classroom learning.

One problem that teachers identified was that many students with a PC of their own preferred to work at home, rather than at school. This confirms many of the observations made by students themselves during the surveys. The reasons given by such students related to the amount of control which they had over their work environment at home, rather than at school. Whilst many of the examples referred to perceived limitations of school hardware and software, the amount of time which students could devote to work at home was also a factor. (See student comments in Appendix 2.)

Students without a home PC are doubly disadvantaged in these circumstances. First, they are dependent on school ICT resources if they need to produce IT-based work. They have far less time which they can devote to its production, and far less freedom to experiment with a range of possible approaches. Second, given that in many schools the number of available computers is less than the number of pupils in the class, teachers allocate computers to those without one at home. This requires a range of tasks to be set to accommodate those who have computers at home: those dependent on school computers miss this additional work.

What the use of computers by students does, however, is to throw these issues into relief. They are central to the ways in which students learn, and are taught. They provide a focus for the ways in which teachers assess work.

The most significant issue, however, is the way in which productive capital, cultural capital, symbolic capital and educational capital are converging. Computers have become the site of conflict on which the class battles of the information age will be fought. Changes in employment patterns during the past decade have resulted in a growth of service-sector jobs, many of which require ICT capability. A flexible labour market requires transferable key skills such as communication, application of number, information technology, problem solving, working with others and improving one's own learning and performance. Dependence on limited institutional resources, education and training will do little for students whose only asset is labour.

Ways in which students work and learn with computers are examined in the next section. Detailed student responses can be found in: Appendix One: Coursework and Marks, and Appendix Two: What is the Mind? How does it work?

Reflections

The most significant aspect of the results was the acceptance, on the part of teachers, of the disparity between the processes and abilities of students and teachers in using computers, and the conceptual gap with Information and Communications Technologies. Many teachers assumed that, because students could do things with computers, they knew how to do them and why they did them. Further, there was an assumption on the part of many teachers that there was one way of doing something – the 'right' way. They were privileging their students as 'experts' and destabilising the ecology of the classroom.

This was matched by an unwillingness by teachers to take charge of the technology for themselves. In part this was because many secondary school teachers still felt that ICT was a separate subject and was not part of their curriculum responsibilities. In part it was also due to the sense of fatigue felt by many teachers who struggled to keep pace with the remorseless flow of curriculum change and documentation visited upon schools.

In addition, a significant number of teachers felt that the disadvantage of those without access to a PC at home could be ameliorated by creating a computer-free zone in their classroom. A sub-text to this was the low level of ownership among teachers themselves. The purchase of a new computer represented a considerable proportion of their disposable income. Those teachers who used computers both at school and home, for a range of tasks, were more likely to be enthusiastic about using ICT in innovative ways within the curriculum. This is supported by the recent findings of Preston, Cox and Cox (2000) for the Teacher Training Agency. The Computers for Teachers scheme, introduced in January 2000, was an attempt to meet this need. A significant number of teachers, however, failed to take up the scheme and viewed it with suspicion.

Using the information

As I looked at the results of the surveys, talked to students and felt the currents shifting in my own classes I was aware that I may be looking in the wrong direction; trying to make sense of the wrong signs. I was looking at what the students were producing, expecting to see an increase in the number of transactional reports and the quantity of data being analysed. I realised that the greatest change was in the way these objects were being produced, and the changing student attitudes towards them. Students could do things with computers, but there was no guarantee that they knew how to do them in a systematic way, or could repeat their work. What was uncertain was whether or not students possessed a mental model of the processes in the systems they were using (Hagmann, Mayer and Nenniger, 1998). Knowing why they did them, as a series of routines that formed part of operational procedures, was difficult to establish. Part of this difficulty may well have been the difference between being able to do something, and analysing and describing the process. However, many students felt that they worked intuitively, and that their computer 'made it work'.

Students knew that there were a number of ways in which tasks could be undertaken: their computers could achieve the same outcome through a number of routines. Their teachers, however, often assumed that there was one way of doing something. The authority of the teacher was being further undermined.

6   Multi-tasking cyborgs: Implications

Connections

The volume of evidence that was collected suggested that an initial hypothesis, that students would produce transactional and analytical work in greater quantity, was only true for those subjects which expected it: Business Studies, Economics, Geography, some Science projects and technology. Perhaps the most significant factor, however, was the way in which these objects were produced. Many students were producing work without feeling that they needed to master programs and operating systems beforehand. They were, in a very real sense, 'just-in-time' workers. Teachers supplied the tasks; they supplied the ideas; the computer made it all work.

Working with computers

The surveys of student computer use from 1995 onwards showed the extent to which a significant number of students used personal computers. Student comments indicated the range of activities for which these machines were used. Indeed, many students commented that they regarded schoolwork, learning and computers as synonymous. Reference has been made to these comments earlier in the study. Their significance, however, is such that they bear repeating again.

Additional material can be found in Appendix One and Appendix Two.

> Now I use my computer for all the work I do apart from Maths and things like that. I can draw on my computer, make music, listen to music, write stories, look up words to find a meaning for it like a dictionary, print out any work I want for homework. I think it makes homework a lot easier because of all the different programs.
>
> (Girl, Year 9.)

This student has created a working environment with her computer, which provides her with the tools and support necessary for the work she produces to be a reflection of her capabilities. Her abilities are augmented and enhanced by the tools which she uses.

> Computers can make homework need a lot more time, even if you're very good at using them, because you end up spending a lot of time tweaking your work. The end product can look very good, especially with expert use. Spellchecks and automatic language aids such as Thesaurus help your writing. Computers with reference software, such as "Encarta" are great for research. AmiPro2 is the best word processor/d.t.p. program in the world. Apart from AmiPro3. You can also sharpen up your brains playing games such as Tetris and Doom.
>
> (Boy, Year 10.)

The judgements made by this boy focus on what is done - the homework, and the fact that more time is spent on it - and how it is done. The awareness of 'expert use' of software and its built-in tools is that it enhances the product. The sub-text is that the user is enhanced: '*You can also sharpen up your brains ...*' The computer-human interface is part of his discourse.

> I had my first computer when I was six. I've used one ever since.
>
> (Boy, Year 12.)

The human-computer interaction described here has been a constant theme in the surveys conducted during the period of this study. As the technology has become more powerful, flexible and sophisticated, so it has become more open to being customised by student users. Individual needs and circumstances have enabled a constantly evolving setup and use of the equipment. Students regard the layout and look of the Graphical User Interface as both a reflection of, and extension to, their personality. In this sense then, if no other, they have taken on attributes of cyborgs.

'Cyborgs'

The image of the cyborg as a super-human combination of the mortal and technology has been part of popular culture for more than twenty years. The term 'cyborg' was initially coined to describe human enhancement: a man-machine system, or hybrid, that would be necessary to survive in, and adapt to, the extra-terrestrial environments of space flight. Routine checks and monitoring would be undertaken automatically, so that the human would be free to create, think, feel and explore (Clynes and Kline, 1960). Cyborgs can also be seen as the tangled networks of meat, metal and technologies that we have become: creatures in a world that is post-gender (Haraway, 1985).

The integration with technology enables humans to transcend their corporeal limitations. This is true for individuals fitted with prosthetic limbs; with heart pacemakers or whose use of pharmaceuticals enables them to overcome bodily malfunction. Science fiction fantasies on television and film, such as The Six Million Dollar Man, Terminator or Robocop, provide a leitmotif for the concerns of our age in much the same way as Frankenstein served for the Enlightenment. Cyborgs, then, provide a route for us to stand aside from the limitations imposed on our bodies by restrictions of race, gender, class and socio-economic status.

The students in this study can be regarded as having integrated with computer technology because the operations which they undertake using the machines have been internalised. That is to say, the programs and routines that they use, they use intuitively. The hardware and the software which they use is seen as a means to an end. They are a tool, a vehicle for combining motor skills, language, images and symbolic manipulation through practical activities. They are enabled to stand aside from the limitations imposed on them as subordinates in the school system.

So computers are the tool, the vehicle for combining motor skills, language, images and symbolic manipulation through practical activities. These practical activities reflect a series of often complex thought processes. They represent a cultural tool that enables the mediation of thought (Wertsch, 1998). The technology enables these processes to be amplified and developed in ways which reflect the integration of technology. Fast multi-tasking has become one indicator of this integration. The students may fail to reflect media images of Cyborgs such as Robocop or the Terminator, but their behaviour and artefacts, products of that behaviour, suggest that the myth is manifesting itself. Computing technology has transformed student expectation of what is possible: the limit is perceived to be that of the technology itself.

A survey of 918 students aged 12-18 showed that a comparatively small percentage listed computers either as ways in which they learned or as ways through which they should learn. This is perhaps not so surprising as it might seem. The extent of computer use would suggest that most students do not regard computers as a subject, something which has to be learned. This compares with the concerns of teachers, who in many cases feel themselves to be in need of training so that they may teach their students about computers: Information Technology, rather than information technology.

Table 6.1: Learning with computers

Year	Student uses a computer for learning			Student thinks that computers should be used for learning		
	Female	Male	All	Female	Male	All
12	30%	50%	40%	6%	0%	3%
10	13%	22%	17%	3%	8%	5%
9	0%	10%	5%	2%	3%	2%
8	4%	13%	8%	9%	14%	12%
7	11%	8%	9%	3%	8%	5%

The high level of response for Years 12 and 10 are attributable to Internet use, specifically cited as an information resource and a way of learning. Other instances cited were linked to the multimedia encyclopedia on CD-ROM, Encarta. Those students who thought that computers should be used for learning gave as their reasons the availability of information on the Internet, and the way in which work could be done individually on the computer. There was no mention of online learning and virtual schools. Whether or not students see schools and learning as synonymous, they do not perceive schools as being 'virtual'.

These figures support statements made by students throughout the surveys, that learning to use their computers is a by-product of using them: they are 'learning how', rather than 'learning about': the learning is how to achieve what the student wants to achieve.

Cyberspace

'Cyberspace' is a term that originated in science fiction to describe virtual worlds. Its most common use, however, is to describe a range of aspects of everyday life connected with computers and the Internet. The use of electronic mail, Internet chat rooms and discussion groups and participation in virtual communities have all contributed to a culture in which simulation is accepted as part of the experience which constitutes the post-modern condition. Electronic data transmission enables 'cashless' economies and purchases; online games provide challenges against opponents whose identity exists only on the screen.

An alternative interpretation of cyberspace is that of an ideology, for those who see themselves as transcending the limitations imposed on them by the society in which they live (Virilio, P. 1995). This concept of cyberspace is seen as a way of being in contact with a global community in which links can be established with those who share the same interests or apparently think in the same way. Those who see themselves as part of cyberspace have a sense of power, endowed by the exclusivity of the skills and concepts shared by the global community. They regard themselves as the cutting edge of technology. This power is reinforced by the anonymity of cyberspace and the apparent lack of temporal responsibility and accountability.

The individuals who are empowered by possession of computer communications see themselves as technological superheroes, moving from one part of the globe to another in nanoseconds. Access to information (whether real or imagined) is what differentiates technoheroes - Virilio's term for what many young people consider to be cyborgs - from the rest of humanity. The structures of inequality are compounded by the continual and rapid updating of hardware, software and the skills and concepts with which they are associated.

When these changes are coupled with increased investment in new communications technologies by business and industry the substitution of the economic factors of labour by capital further disenfranchises those who lack the skills needed to exploit new possibilities.

Technoheroes reify this constant advance: the latest upgrades, the latest skills and the latest vocabulary are all essential to staying ahead: having the edge needed to ride the InfoWave. Students adopt these rapid technical developments as another facet of their perception that life is a process of constant change.

> Computers are the future they are quick and easy.
>
> (Boy, Year 9.)

Table 6.2: Changes in the cost of computer memory

Average price per megabyte of computer memory (US$)

1988	1989	1990	1991	1992	1993	1994	1995	1996	1997	1998	1999 (est)	2000 (est)
$11.54	$9.30	$6.86	$5.23	$3.00	$1.46	$.705	$.33	$.179	$.101	$.068	$.039	$.027

Source: Porter, J. (1998)

This constant change can be demonstrated in Table 6.2, which illustrates the dramatic fall in the price of computer memory. (This smooth progression conveniently ignores the spikes caused by surges in demand, earthquakes in Taiwan and other glitches of globalisation.) The sub-text is the dramatic increase in the demand for computer memory by software packages. Over the past five years the price of a computer package has remained relatively stable: what has changed is the level of specification available for the price that is paid. The concept of 'more for your money' drives people to upgrade their machines with increasing regularity.

> Computers are expensive but if you didn't have one you probably would be degraded because of it in later life.
>
> (Boy, Year 10.)

The comment used by this student in his letter was reflected by a number of others, who saw computers as creating added value in their schoolwork, which would then lead to greater opportunities for progression. It perhaps reflects the post-industrial nature of Leeds, in which employment in the secondary sector of production, manufacturing, has been in steady decline for the past twenty five years. The biggest employment area is in the service sector, more specifically in the banking, insurance and financial sectors.

Computers and enjoyment

Many students have commented that they enjoy working on the computer. A number have described it as 'fun'. Whilst this may, in part, be due to the fact that they can listen to music and play games whilst they are working, other factors should be taken into account to explain the element of 'fun' and enjoyment.

The focus of many consumer electronic technologies has been on ludic elements: that is to say, aspects of games and play. Early surveys of student computer use revealed an ambiguity as to what constituted a computer, especially among younger students. Many mentioned games consoles or hand-held electronic games. Commodore Amiga computers had been purchased in the hope that they would offer both a platform for sophisticated games playing and a tool for schoolwork.

These elements of play have been incorporated into mainstream applications, most specifically as icons, prompts and Wizards. Indeed, many programs offer animated initial screens as a way into the content. Whilst these were first targeted at younger users (as in Microsoft's Creative Writer and Creative Artist) they have spread to other programs (for example, that for Epson Stylus colour printers). The development of the Graphical User Interface (GUI) presents the computer user with an interface that initially simulates the space on a desktop. The user can then customise the space by installing short-cuts to favourite programs and document folders, personalising the screen-savers: in short, making the machine a reflection of the user's personality.

The GUI also presents an opaque interface with the computer: there is no necessity to learn sets of commands and then use these to instruct the machine. The user points at 'objects' and clicks to activate them: on-screen Wizards supply questions, prompts and instructions to enable users to achieve their purpose. Students can point and click at programs, documents and objects; switch from one to another; perform one task whilst another is running in the background.

Multi-tasking

The conventional understanding of multi-tasking is that of a computer running a number of programs simultaneously. One program will run in the foreground (a word-processor), whilst others run in the background - a print manager printing a number of documents; a database indexing a datafile. Other programs will foreground themselves: email announcements; error messages from the operating system; 'paper out' reports from the print manager. Other instances of multi-tasking occur when students have a number of windows open on the screen and switch from one document to another as they are working.

Comments from students in previous sections have illustrated their use of multi-tasking capabilities whilst they work with their machines. One way in which students switch from one task to another is the combination of the ALT/TAB keys. This enables a number of programs to run and the students to move between them. Observation suggests four main ways in which this technique is used.

The most frequently observed use of this technique is when students switch between programs and applications as part of the task - with a spreadsheet and a word-processor; a web page, a word-processor and a presentation program or between a document and a CD-ROM.

Another use is cited during homework, particularly coursework for GCSE. Students will have a number of tasks open, and switch between them as they become tired, or become stuck.

The third use is an extension of toggling between programs, where they will switch from the tasks to a game, and then back again. These uses all demonstrate the way in which students move from full engagement with the task (and learning) to a state of reflection. Whilst this reflection may take place during a period of 'tinkering' with the text, by changing fonts and margins, running the spell-check and other utilities, it also takes place whilst the student engages with other tasks, or plays a game.

The final use of switching is between licit and illicit activities, when students are expected to be on task but occupy themselves instead with the maintenance of their web site, speculative surfing or with interactive chat rooms. The most ingenious collective use of the ALT/TAB facility was with a class which was being taught Excel spreadsheet routines. The teacher was demonstrating the program and the tasks the students were expected to undertake. The students were using their own chat program to carry on 'conversations' totally unrelated to the lesson. When the teacher asked a question, or moved around the room the student would ALT/TAB from the chat to the spreadsheet (Abbott, 1998). It might be argued that multi-tasking is merely the material form of an activity that has always taken place. What the computer offers to the user, however, is the prospect of simultaneity, however much of a simulation that might be. Simultaneity becomes embodied, both within the computer and its user. As Gardner has commented,

> The invention of the computer has provided a powerful if ever-changing model of cognition and an invaluable tool in simulation, data analysis and conceptualisation of the human Mind.
>
> (Gardner, 1993, p.41.)

This use of the computer as a metaphor for the human Mind and cognition is one that is explored in the next section.

Learning styles

Learning styles are the different ways in which individuals think and learn. These become formalised as expectations and behaviour, which the individual then brings to the task of learning. The stages of learning can be separated into three broad areas: cognition, the acquisition of knowledge; conceptualisation, the processing of knowledge and the affective factors related to these. The focus is therefore on the process of learning.

Kolb (1984) saw learning as an active process. Its stages formed a continuum, from concrete experience: (involvement); reflective observation, watching others or developing observations about one's own experience; through abstract conceptualization: the creation of theories to explain one's observations; to active experimentation, using theories to solve problems and make decisions.

Gardner (1983) identified different types of learning, particularly those characterised as 'know-how' and 'know that'. From that he defined 'multiple intelligences', to describe the different ways (and combinations of ways) in which individuals learn. Learning can be seen as 'playing' with different capabilities: the verbal/linguistic; logical/mathematical; visual/spatial; musical/rhythmic; bodily/kinesthetic; social/interpersonal and personal. This perspective provides an immediate rationale for the use of computers by young people: the combination of play elements – the ludic – the use of language as part of the process, together with visual stimulus, means that the computer provides a focus for different types of learning.

Some, however, assume that the young learner - a child - is not the same as a mature learner - an adult, and that the learning styles must be different (Knowles, 1970). Adult learners are often characterised as autonomous and self-directed; goal oriented; problem centred and needing to know why the learning is taking place. Adults are seen as practical problem solvers, able to draw on accumulated life experience. The young learner, the child, is assumed to possess few, if any, of these characteristics. Many of the assumptions implicit in classroom praxis are predicated on this dichotomy.

Learning strategies for adult learners have been grouped in binary terms by Felder and Soloman (1998). They have re-worked Gardner's concept of multiple intelligences into descriptions of active and reflective learners; sensing and intuitive learners; visual and verbal learners and sequential and global learners. Indeed, Gardner comments that

> …intuitive theories remain as pre-potent ways of knowing and are likely to re-emerge with full force once the person leaves a scholastic milieu.
>
> (1993, p.86.)

The point is made that computers are artefacts that reinforce intuitive understanding and ways of knowing and learning. This perspective places computers as tools, external to, although enhancing, cognitive processes and development.

Multi-tasking and learning

This research has indicated the diversity of approaches utilised by students when working with computers. Further, the extent to which students use them for work illustrates the ways in which the computers are not simply artefacts that reinforce intuitive understanding and ways of knowing, but rather an integration with the understanding and the thought processes. Knowledge is therefore constructed by the learner, as part of the work process.

If the picture of an adult learner is one of someone autonomous and self-directed; goal oriented; problem centred and needing to know why the learning is taking place; a practical problem solver, able to draw on accumulated life experience, how is that different from the way in which young (child) learners work with their computers?   The opportunities for learning commonly applied to adult learners, those of case studies, role play, simulations and self evaluation are precisely those through which younger students learn when using their computers.

Multi-tasking cyborgs?

What differentiates computers from previous technology to which students have had access, such as cassette recorders, calculators or VCR machines is that both the software and hardware offer a seemingly endless range of possibilities. Whether the student is an active or reflective learner; a sensing or intuitive individual; a visual or verbal learner and sequential or global learners, the way in which the computer is used will reflect that. The active, visual, intuitive and global nature of multi-tasking is likely to develop those particular styles of learning. Conventional educational pedagogy has been superceded by learners who have constructed the active, goal-directed learning patterns previously associated with adults. The integration of computers with the individual's understanding and thought processes will create new ways of thinking.

The cyborg of Clynes and Kline constructs itself with every new piece of work. The student and her computer form the man-machine system, the hybrid, the cyborg. The operating system and the programs perform the routine checks and monitoring, checking, correcting, formatting, saving the work. The student is set free from her limitations, to create, to think and to explore a range of possibilities.

Just as long as she is one of the 80% with access to a computer at home.

Snapshots and surprises

By the time I had finished this section I felt that I had identified a pattern of working that a significant number of students were adopting. I had almost five thousand responses to surveys over a four-year period. The problem was whether the themes emerging from student responses were simply descriptions of behaviour, or whether there was a more fundamental change. In part, it was the problem of the Uses and Gratifications approach to data collection, and the tracking of responses in percentage terms. What I still lacked was the evidence that the students as cyborgs were using their computers as the tools to set them free.

I had assumed that the most immediately apparent impact of computers on student work, the ability to handle, manipulate and present data within documents, would be the factors that would have increased. I had some ten years of student work to analyse. Whilst my assumption was true for the first three or four years of the work sample, there was no significant increase in the evidence beyond this point.

It was as if those students whose approach to work was analytical and systematic were able to produce more of it, and those whose limitations held them back from producing this type of work had been facilitated by computers. After that, more students were using computers, but for different purposes, in different ways.

The rapid take-up of computers by students had certainly changed what they did; it had changed the ways in which they talked about computers and work. What was more problematic, however, was whether or not they had changed the ways in which they thought. I decided to investigate the ways in which students conceived of the Mind: I felt that their responses might enable me to identify the influence of computers on their thinking.

7   Concepts of Mind: A developmental picture

Introduction

The surveys, student comments and observations undertaken during the course of the research suggested that patterns of cognition and learning were emerging that differed from conventional models of cognitive development and learning theory. A plausible hypothesis was that prolonged exposure to computers and the language associated with them would contribute to the metaphor of information-processing being applied to the ways in which students perceived Mind and associated processes.

One way of assessing whether these changes had manifested themselves within the student population was to test their concepts of Mind. If the 'computer as brain' analogy had been accepted by a number of students one would expect to see this reflected in the ways in which they defined the Mind. It could be expected that this would also be reflected in the ways in which students worked. In the next phase of the research, therefore, students were asked to define the human Mind, and how it worked.

Theoretical background

Much of the educational process is predicated on the assumption that learning and competence is developmental: the building blocks of knowledge require sound foundations if the ultimate structure is to be solid. In *The Philosophy of Childhood* Matthew (1994) examined the philosophical discourse of children, elicited through the use of Socratic questioning. His findings suggested that the philosophy of childhood should be treated as an area separate from that of mainstream philosophy, rather than as an emergent pre-adult philosophy. If this childhood phase is separate from what we conventionally expect to be philosophy then we cannot describe it as the first stage in a developmental process. The developmental stages identified by Piaget (1952; 1959), Kohlberg (1969) and others would apparently not apply to one aspect of thought.

Matthew examined the First Causes of conceptual development, to determine when concepts emerged and when they changed. His thesis was that if children could no longer be seen as miniature adults, they may considered pre-rational or pre-scientific beings. If that was the case, then it might be considered that they could not be thought of in the same terms as those who were adult, rational and scientific. Implicit in this is, of course, the model of 'human' as adult, rational and scientific. This serves as the model for much of the teaching and learning process in schools, in which children are led through sequences (related to their developmental phase) to the rational and scientific state that is adulthood.

Evidence of Modality Judgements demonstrated by children when watching television would suggest that the concept of personality and existence is something which children do possess. When children see themselves or others recorded on video they engage with the concept of what constitutes 'live'. Work by Jaglom and Gardner (1981) suggests that there are three levels of modality judgement through which children pass up to the age of 5. They use the structuralist terms paratactic and hypotactic to describe the processes undertaken by children. Paratactic means that within a structure, options exist alongside each other - for example, within a compound sentence, where elements are linked by the conjunction 'and'. A hypotactic structure, on the other hand, is one with subordinate elements - for example, a compound sentence with embedded clauses.

Modality judgement	Process	Age
Non-differentiation.		⇨2 years.
Sharp differentiation.	Binary paratactic structures.	
Re-integration.	Complex hypotactic structures.	⇨5 years.

This raises the question as to whether children are working towards higher stages of developmental concepts, grappling with category and conceptual errors until they are resolved. Or are they rather, as Matthew suggests, exploring different and, to them, equally satisfying theories from which they move on or move away?

What does appear to happen is that children constantly reconstruct their concepts. This builds their understanding of the world. As concepts are constantly reconstructed the cognitive process changes and develops. Cognitive development is therefore endogenous. With this cognitive growth comes a theoretical shift in the way in which objects (and the relationships between them) are conceptualised. This has an impact on the use of language (cf. Winograd and Flores) and the use of language (which can be regarded as one of Vygotsky's 'intellectual tools') in turn has an impact on the cognitive process.   When young people are exposed to theoretical terms and expressions ('cognates') this triggers a conceptual search for meaning.

Gopnik and Melzoff, 1997, view this process as analagous to that followed by scientists, where existing theory is reviewed in the light of experience.   This theory and its postulates have implications which are themselves tested against experience.   In the light of these there is a reorganization of ideas, which then results in a new theory.

Gopnik and Melzoff argue that each child at birth is equipped with a set of dedicated interpretative devices, or modules.   These enable children to construct and develop a variety of mini-theories of the world around them, in terms of animate and inanimate, real and non-real, cause and effect, and so on. This is the process that they see as similar to that undertaken by scientists. The concept of the Language Acquisition Device (Chomsky, 1968) would be a precondition for the interpretative devices posited by Gopnik and Melzoff.

Emerging theories of Mind

The assumption underlying this phase of the research was that responses cited by students in their definitions of Mind would be informed by a range of influences.   Many of these would be drawn from popular science and the media.   Three separate strands emerge from these influences, which could be termed Constructivist, Materialist and Computational.

The Constructivist strand would hold that the Mind is a product of our biology, combined with the five senses, basic drives and the capacity to learn.   It has evolved culturally, with built-in replication from generation to generation, and is shaped by arbitrary societal variances. Our behaviour is predicated by both biology and culture, whereas our constraints are imposed by biology.

The Materialist model of Mind would suggest that the Mind is produced by the brain, through the psycho-chemical properties of brain and tissue.   What we sometimes call 'Mind' is therefore nothing more than a consequence of the brain's anatomy and physiology.

The interpretation of Mind that could be termed Computational is based on information theory – encoding and decoding – so our beliefs, desires and information are encoded as symbols.   The congruence between symbols generates new symbols (our beliefs, desires and information) and some of these symbols will generate a physical reaction, which we term behaviour.

Congruent symbols group together in modules: these mental modules can act together (a process often referred to as 'chunking' (McShane, 1991, pp.342-343), producing an infinite number of different representations. The different levels of generality of these representations are the cognitive process. These 'mental tools' can be content-free, which offers the power to think and behave in new ways.

Differences in thinking will lead to differences in encoding (symbol generation), which in turn will produce differences in congruence. When this occurs the result will be new symbols (beliefs). These new beliefs will lead to differences in behaviour.

The Computational theory of Mind informed the perspective of Winograd and Flores. It formed part of the grounding for this investigation.

Investigating concepts of Mind

During 1996-97 two investigations were undertaken to determine which concepts of Mind were held by young people, and how they were formed. The first was carried out by A/S Psychology students at Boston Spa Comprehensive School as part of their coursework and an introduction to data collection techniques. The group decided on the single question What is the Mind? and asked a random sample of twelve students in each year group. (Total: 72 students. School roll: 1787 students.)

Results were collated and a range of responses was identified.

Table 7.1: Investigating concepts of Mind

Response	Year 7	Year 8	Year 9	Year 10	Year 11	Year 12/13
Don't know	6	4	3			
The brain/grey matter	1	1	2	3	6	3
For thinking	2	5	3	1		2
For storage	1					1
Intelligence	1					
For control	1			1	3	
Personality			2	6		2
Consciousness			2	1		4
A computer					1	
A major organ					1	

By Year 10 all of the students interviewed were able to attempt a definition of the Mind.   What this initial survey failed to reveal was whether students in Years 7-9 who were unable to provide a definition of the Mind lacked the concept of Mind, or lacked the language through which they could express otherwise inchoate concepts.   One reason may be more fundamental, in that, whilst many students have an implicit understanding of how and why they do things, they are unable to explain why (Cf. Piaget; Vygotsky).   Donaldson (1987) and Gardner (1983) argue that the form of the question posed by the researcher predicates the response, rather than the level of understanding in the learner.

It was significant that only after Year 10 did students identify the Mind with personality or consciousness, whereas the Year 11 students interviewed primarily saw the Mind as being connected with the Brain, with thinking and with control.   For almost 20% of students in the sample the Mind was synonymous with the Brain.

Metaphors of the Mind

It was anticipated that the students would construct their explanations of the Mind from the language and concepts that they used for other things - most specifically, from the language and concepts of the computers which they use every day.   What was significant, however, is that only one student from the sample (in Year 11) compared the Mind to a computer. Whilst the computer may be an information processing device, and the Mind process information, students did not see the two as synonymous. Another student (in the same year) described the Mind as "…a major organ…".   Students in the initial sample, then, did not consider the Mind and the computer as synonymous.

Nearly 30% of students, however, considered the Mind in functional terms: for thinking, for storage, for intelligence or for control - the information processing model.   There is a correlation here with responses from students in an earlier survey, (Uses and Gratifications Survey, Spring 1995) when they were asked why they used computers.   The responses grouped as Personal Identity included the set Reality Exploration, in which students cited gaining mastery of computer routines as an important reason for their use of computers.   This transactional understanding of the ways in which computers are used may well have provided the students with a model for understanding the Mind.

Testing the hypotheses

During the summer term of 1997 a new survey was constructed which extended to the whole school, to identify models of Mind held by students, determine a developmental progression and test the validity of the Computational model as an explanation for the questions "What is the Mind? How does it work?". All responses were recorded, analyzed and grouped by age and gender. (Years 11 and 13 did not form part of this survey: they were on study leave.)

Students produced a number of definitions and examples within their responses. These have been recorded within each of the relevant categories.

Table 7.2: What is the Mind?

Year group ⇒	Y7		Y8		Y9		Y10		Y12	
Gender:	F	M	F	M	F	M	F	M	F	M
F= 533; M= 521	128	103	112	107	134	113	115	114	36	72
Category ⇓	%	%	%	%	%	%	%	%	%	%
Control	67	59	49	46	51	46	50	31	47	19
Brain	51	50	35	27	31	34	38	33	53	11
Thinking	34	28	51	40	51	42	26	23	47	17
Storage	25	28	28	42	32	26	19	19	25	8
Emotion	24	11	38	24	36	35	30	20	56	15
Ethics	11	9	10	2	7	7	10	4	17	7
Identity	10	12	27	15	20	4	22	21	44	14
Computer	8	16	4	10	9	13	3	4		7
A major organ	6	3	4	6	7	5	3	3	6	1
Mechanical	6	4			4	6				1
Intellect	5	1	2		1.5	2	3	1		
Consciousness	5	5		2	4	1	5	9	11	11
Communication	4	1			2	7	2	1	3	3
Visualisation					1	2		1		
An Inner Voice			1	3	2	1			6	
The Soul			3	3	4	4			3	4
God/Supernatural			2	2				2		
A Myth, Dream, Abstraction					1			1		
A Way of Thinking									8	1
Achievement							1			
Power			1				1	1		
Don't know			1	1			8	11		1

Student responses

Student responses to the questions tended to be thoughtful and considered. This is particularly true for the younger students, many of whom found it difficult to articulate their ideas. Nevertheless, they tried to communicate their understanding, whilst recognising that their ideas could not yet be considered fully formed. Many resorted to diagrams and illustrations in their explanations.

The number of students in Year 10 (8% female; 11% male) who responded with a 'Don't know' may be indicative of a developmental shift that is observed between Year 9 and Year 10.

One Year 7 student wrote the following account of his understanding of the Mind. It extends over three paragraphs. The only editing is where my comments are interspersed.

> The human Mind is, to put it bluntly, just a collection of millions of cells, making a kind of pinky-grey blob inside our heads. However, it is also the amazing thing that helps (and makes) us think and live our lives differently from all the other animals on earth. Every human being is unique - no two are exactly the same. We have evolved further than anyone could imagine, from monkey-like beings in the beginning to the most clever race on earth, with huge cities and modern technology. Although we are all unique, we are not, however, all equal. Many people on our earth live in poverty, whilst others recline in the lap of luxury.

The initial paragraph establishes a socio-biological foundation for what follows. The Mind is reduced to the interactions of a collection of cells ('millions') located in the brain ('a kind of pinky-grey blob'). It produces individual thought that leads to difference and development, whilst at the same time producing inequality and justice.

> The human Mind is an incredible, almost incomprehensibly complicated thing. It controls every movement and thought of a human, from breathing to driving a car. It can remember things that happened way back in the past, and take in new information and learn new skills every day.

At this point other aspects of the Mind are identified: control, memory and information processing. This latter aspect is developed in the final paragraph.

> Basically, it works by a complex system of nerves and cells to send messages around the body, telling us what to do. The cells in the brain

control movement, memory and all other functions of our bodies. The body is able to sense things with the nerves, such as heat and cold, and these can send pictures to the brain which tells us what we are seeing. Human beings can also hear sounds, smell and feel.

(Boy, Year 7.)

The information processing metaphor becomes fully developed at this point – "…sends messages around the body, telling us what to do." In the final phase, though, it is the brain which "tells us what we are seeing."

The student here attempts to construct an explanation of Mind that combines the three popular explanations: the Constructivist: "…live our lives differently…we have evolved further than anyone could imagine…we are all unique"; through the Materialist: " just a collection of millions of cells a complex system of nerves and cells…" to the Computational explanation: " it controls every movement and thought…remember things…take in new information…learn new skills…" It is the explanation of a twelve-year-old who knows that the understanding of Mind depends upon the perspective one adopts. The process of definition itself constructs the Mind.

A simple explanation of Mind, in that it is immaterial and both the cause and product of consciousness, combines elements of both the constructivist and materialist approaches.

If you cut open our heads you wouldn't be able to find our Mind. It is not an organ.

(Girl, Year 8.)

Everyone has a Mind. It starts as a baby when you are born and goes when you die.

(Girl, Year 8.)

There isn't an organ in your body called The Mind, it's just inside.

(Girl, Year 8.)

Some explanations are reminiscent of Berkeley's Idealism or phenomenalism.

The Mind is in our heads, and without it nothing would exist.

(Girl, Year 9.)

The human Mind is a concept called consciousness.

(Girl, Year 9.)

Other explanations acknowledge the inherent tension between materialist and constructivist definitions, whilst adding the possibility of an existentialist dimension.

> The human Mind is probably one of the most complicated, if not the most complicated 'thing' on earth. Some people may say the Mind is the brain, but the brain is different to the Mind. It doesn't work like a computer or robot, where you switch it on or off, it's just there, inside you, all the time, and nobody can change it or take it away. People say "I've changed my Mind" not my brain. This is because they have changed their opinion and feelings on a certain subject: this is their Mind.
>
> (Boy, Year 9.)

Here the student starts from a position of Mind-body dualism, acknowledging that the materialist position based on computing cannot provide an adequate explanation. For him, the Mind is constructed from thoughts, opinions and feelings. Another student, also in Year 9, is less able to articulate her explanation. She is aware that an understanding of Mind is essentially developmental. For her, however, Mind and identity are one and the same.

> When I was younger, I would have said that the Mind is like a box, which opens and closes according to the situation. It lets out different emotions, words, thoughts etc. But now I cannot even think about what the Mind is, without getting myself confused. The Mind makes us what we are. Without your Mind, you have no outside, because there is nothing on the inside.
>
> (Girl, Year 9.)

The following comments illustrate the beginnings of existential awareness; "the ghost in the machine", to paraphrase Koestler.

> The human Mind is two things. It is a complex organ made up of millions of little cells. In other words, it is a part of your brain. The other thing, it is something that is there but not there.
>
> (Girl, Year 10.)

> The human Mind is not matter, it is abstract concept which binds our interior thoughts and impulses to our exterior actions. It is not there yet it is a window to our soul which lets our emotions have a playground of instincts. It is the nucleus of our existential body of Mind and matter.
>
> (Boy, Year 10.)

Other explanations cast the Mind as 'the midwife of change':

It's like a time bomb, waiting to go off.

(Boy, Year 10.)

The human Mind is the driving force for mankind's thinking, as individuals and as a collective. It works on instinct and experience.

(Boy, Year 10.)

The predominant explanations given by students fall into two categories: the first is that of consciousness, both as its cause and its product. The second is that of the activity of the brain: the interaction of cells and body chemistry.

It holds memory, and builds personality through experience and learning.

(Boy, Year 10.)

The human Mind is a series of impulses generated by the central nervous system of the brain.

(Boy, Year 10.)

The human Mind is grey and squashy. It is full of cells and electricity.

(Girl, Year 10.)

The human Mind is what gives us consciousness. It enables us to feel and make decisions, to invent and to create.

(Girl, Year 10.)

Mind is something you can't touch – it has no matter – it is just there and you have to trust and believe it, because there is no proof.

(Girl, Year 12.)

In a way the Mind is a learning experience.

(Girl, Year 12.)

Summary

Student responses to the questions "What is the Mind? How does it work?" illustrate a range of explanations, the majority of which have origins in philosophical enquiry. None of the students tested, however, have received any conventional teaching in the subject. Their education process assumes that building blocks of knowledge lead to concept formation and understanding, and that complex issues such as the philosophy of Mind are dealt with during the tertiary stage of education.

If this is the case, it may be safe to assume that the young people have access to these building blocks of knowledge outside the education system. One source of knowledge may be televised 'popular science' programmes. The Empiricist model of Knowledge, that it is formed through experience, observation and reflection, may provide an explanation of how these concepts form.

It may well be, however, that the concepts have developed endogenously: of themselves as individuals, their consciousness and the world around them, which has produced this understanding. If this is the case, then the tools which the students use may well be responsible for constructing this knowledge.

The most powerful tools which students use are computers, which provide the user with constant feedback about the problem solving, task management and the thinking process. Young users have an interior dialogue with Self: the 'Inner Voice' referred to by some; the 'Brain' and 'Thinking' referred to by so many others.

The frequency of responses that utilise an explanation for the Mind that has an information-processing focus – Mind as Control; as Brain; as Thinking; as Storage, are likely to have their origin in the computers used as tools by the students.

8   Students' Minds

Student responses

Data from the students provided an extremely rich developmental picture of their concepts of Mind. As in previous surveys, students went out of their way to produce thoughtful and illuminating responses. Many wrote their name on the paper and added extra sheets to the response form. Many students provided illustrations to supplement their ideas. All of the responses carried the research forward in productive ways.

Analysis

The analysis of responses in terms of age and gender revealed differences in the way in which the Mind is conceptualised. There would appear to be a disparity in the ways in which female and male students conceive the Mind and the way it works. This is particularly true when responses that can be interpreted as Constructivist are examined. These would suggest that female students have a more developed and complex concept of Mind, and that this is viewed through the perspective of affective terms: as Emotion, Ethics, Identity. Where male students have a stronger response rate is with concepts that could be described as more transactional.

Table 8.1: The constructivist model

	Emotion (% response)		Ethics (% response)		Identity (% response)	
	Female	Male	Female	Male	Female	Male
Y7	24	11	11	9	10	12
Y8	38	24	10	2	27	15
Y9	36	35	7	4	20	4
Y10	30	20	10	4	22	21
Y12	56	15	17	7	44	14

Figure 8.1: The constructivist model of Mind

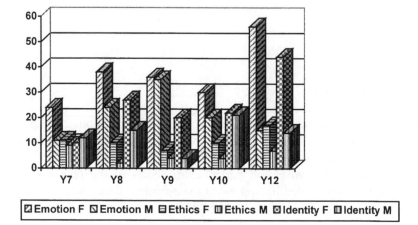

Emotion F   Emotion M   Ethics F   Ethics M   Identity F   Identity M

Table 8.2: Mind as the site of emotion

Emotion
(% response)

	Female	Male
Y7	24	11
Y8	38	24
Y9	36	35
Y10	30	20
Y12	56	15

Figure 8.2: Mind as the site of emotion and feelings

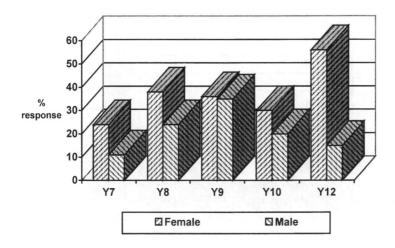

The correlation between the Mind and emotions and feelings is stronger among female than male respondents: female range 24-56%; male range 11-35%. This would contribute to evidence from other responses in this grouping. Young males would appear to have a more transactional approach to affective aspects of Mind, such as Emotion, Ethics and Individual Identity, than their female counterparts.

Table 8.3: Mind as the source of ethics

Ethics
(% response)

	Female	Male
Y7	11	9
Y8	10	2
Y9	7	4
Y10	10	4
Y12	17	7

Figure 8.3: Mind as the source of ethics

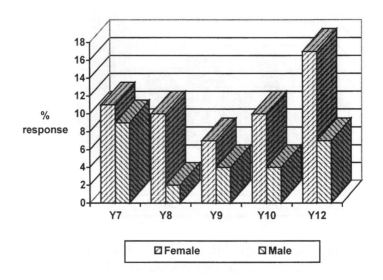

The general frequency of response would suggest that girls are more likely than boys to cite the Mind as the source of ethical standards. This is shown most strongly in Year 12, where 17% of females identify the Mind with holding ethical standards, compared with 7% of males. The female range is 7-17%; male 2-9%. Ethical standards are predominantly viewed here as external, outside the individual and socially determined.

Table 8.4: Mind as the focus of identity

Identity
(% response)

	Female	Male
Y7	10	12
Y8	27	15
Y9	20	4
Y10	22	21
Y12	44	14

Figure 8.4: Mind as an individual's identity

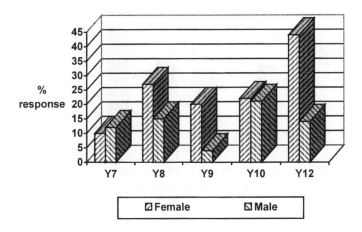

By Year 8 a significant number of girls have linked the Mind with an individual's identity. This link is particularly strong by Year 12 (44%). The male Year 10 response, at 21%, represents the peak. This contrasts identity as a psychological construct for female respondents and as an external social construct for male respondents.

Table 8.5: The Materialist Model

Brain
(% response)

	Female	Male
Y7	51	50
Y8	35	27
Y9	31	34
Y10	38	33
Y12	53	11

Figure 8.5: Mind as synonymous with brain

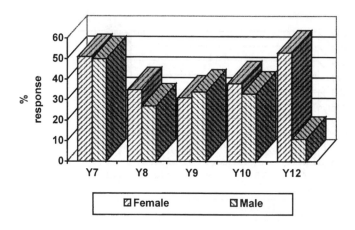

A significant number of students see the Mind and Brain as synonymous. This is particularly true of female students, whose responses fall from Year 7, at 51% to Year 9, at 31%. They then rise again from Year 10, at 38% to Year 12, at 53%. Male responses vary with a peak in Year 7, at 50%, perhaps when there is an awareness of the amount of knowledge that must be processed. Students in Year 7 are just commencing their secondary education, in which the syllabus is constructed of separated strands of knowledge which they have to process - a culture of mystification. Students in Years 9 and 10, on the threshold of GCSE examinations, are aware of their limitations in terms of what they have to know if they are to do well.

The Computational Model

Student responses relating to this model fell into three separate categories. The first, and strongest, saw the Mind as synonymous with the Control of the body and its actions. Thinking explained Mind in terms of the process of thought, whilst Storage saw Mind as the repository of memory.

Table 8.6: Computational Models of Mind

	Control (% response)		Thinking (% response)		Storage (% response)	
	Female	Male	Female	Male	Female	Male
Y7	67	59	34	28	25	28
Y8	49	46	51	40	28	42
Y9	51	46	51	42	32	26
Y10	50	31	26	23	19	19
Y12	47	19	47	17	25	8

Figure 8.6: Computational Models of Mind:
responses by year

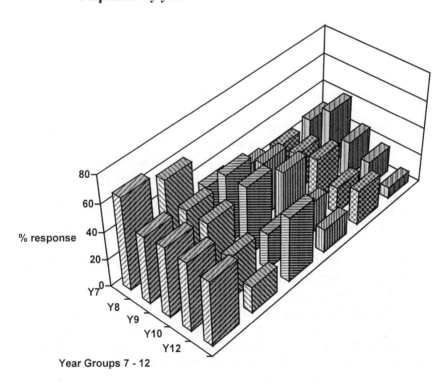

Year Groups 7 - 12

Control F   Control M   Thinking F   Thinking M   Storage F   Storage M

Figure 8.7: Mind as a computer

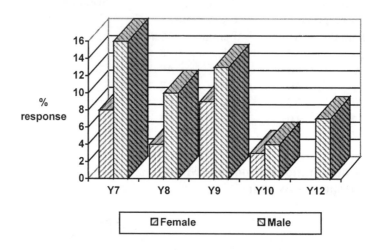

Mind as computer, or a computational Mind?

Whilst the peak response for the concept of the Mind as a computer is Year 7, with 16%, there is a consistent identification of the concept on the part of boys. The strongest response by girls is in Year 9, with only 9%, compared with 13% for Year 9 males. This concept of information processing links with that of the Mind for storage and memory, and that of thinking. No female respondents in Year 12 mentioned the concept. However, the peak response for identification of the Mind with a computer was 16%.

What is of most significance is the response that the Mind is not a computer. A computer was seen as something passive, responding to instructions from a user. Students did not view their Minds as inert, without a program or operating system. On the contrary: they viewed the Mind as active, creative and proactive, rather than merely reactive.

Despite this, the three themes of Control, Thinking and Storage patterned the uses to which computers were put by the students, and the ways in which they used them.

Table 8.7: Metaphysical concepts of the Mind

Year group ⇒	Y7		Y8		Y9		Y10		Y12	
Gender:	F	M	F	M	F	M	F	M	F	M
F= 533; M= 521	128	103	112	107	134	113	115	114	36	72
Category ⇓	%	%	%	%	%	%	%	%	%	%
An Inner Voice			1	3	2	1			6	
The Soul			3	3	4	4			3	4
God/Supernatural			2	2				2		
A Myth, Dream, Abstraction					1				1	

The significance of these figures lies primarily in the low response rate: in other words, some concepts were not mentioned at all. There were no Year 7 responses for any of these themes. Where a correlation between the Mind and God is made this is on three occasions: Year 8, where both boys and girls generated a 2% response, and Year 10, where boys generated a 2% response. It is, perhaps, more illuminating to cite the number of respondents, rather than a percentage response, given that statistics have been rounded. Four students in Year 8 cited God, as did two in Year 10: six students out of more than one thousand surveyed.

The link between the Mind and the Soul generated a response rate of between 3% (Year 8, male and female; Y12 female) and 4% (Year 9, male and female; Year 12 male.) The concept of the Mind as an inner voice is at its strongest with Y12 females (6%), but occurs spasmodically across the age and gender range.

Summary

Of the total number of responses - 1054 students - only 25 responded that they did not know what the Mind was. 97.6% of the total, therefore, were able to attempt a definition. What was significant was the eclectic mix of responses which nevertheless matched the three models outlined at the beginning of this section.

There would appear to be a disparity in the ways in which female and male students conceive the Mind and the way it works. Responses would suggest that female students have a more developed and complex concept of Mind, and that this is viewed primarily in affective terms. Where male students have a stronger response rate is with concepts that could be described as more transactional.

One concept of Mind is cited most frequently by all respondents. It is the Computational Model. This explanation used metaphors drawn from Information Technology: control; memory, information processing. This group views the Mind as responsible for controlling the body; for the thinking process; for the function of memory.

The majority of students do not, however, describe the Mind as a computer. Those who did constituted a small group, and were predominantly male.

Many of the students saw the Mind and brain as synonymous, and conflated the computational model with the Materialist Model of Mind. The concepts of information processing, however, provided the conceptual framework for their explanations.

The Constructivist Model of Mind used as an explanatory framework by students focused on features that could be described as affective, and the most frequently cited attributes were Emotion, Ethics and Identity. Female response rates were considerably higher than those for males.

Metaphysical explanations of Mind were consistently low across the whole school population. It would appear that most students have a range of concepts that they can draw on to attempt an explanation of the Mind and how it works without having to draw on non-rational explanations.

Amongst the 1054 students who responded to the survey the predominant view of the Mind is as an information processing device. In terms of the whole school, 47% saw the Mind as responsible for control of the body; 36% saw the Mind as responsible for thinking and 25% viewed it as memory, the storage of information. Trends in terms of age and gender have already been described. The significance of Winograd and Flores' thesis, that a new technology changes our language, our understanding and the world which we construct, could well be reflected in the ways which this young people conceive themselves and their Minds.

What is more significant, perhaps, is the range of factors which are cited by students as constituting their Mind: the complex and rich patterning that they see as residing 'inside their head'. It is in the application of 'what is inside the head' to what things are made to happen that computers become a significant tool.

Concepts of Mind and multiple intelligences

The thesis that individuals possess multiple intelligences (Gardner, 1983; 1993) is reflected in the ways that the students attempted to define Mind.

Gardner's identification of Linguistic, Musical, Logico-mathematical, Spatial, Bodily-kinaesthetic and Personal intelligences can be seen in the terms that students used.

Gardner	Student description
Linguistic	Communication
Logico-mathematical	The Brain; thinking; information storage.
Bodily-kinaesthetic	A control device; A major organ; Visualisation; Mechanical.
Personal	Emotion; Ethics; identity; Consciousness; The inner voice.

No students linked musical ability with the Mind: neither was the quality of Spatial intelligence mentioned. What is significant is that the qualities that Gardner identifies as contributing to intelligence form the responses which students cited as components of the Mind and the way in which it works.

Conclusion

The Computational Model of Mind may well constitute a contemporary hegemony. If this is the case then it is to be expected that references to such a model in the media, and as a metaphor of common currency, will frame young people's concepts and discourse. It may be that students simply use the tools with which they work as a source of metaphors for understanding. What is undeniable, however, is that their discourse is shaped by these processes.

If the Computational Model of Mind is the dominant interpretation accepted by young people, and if the world which they construct is shaped by this, then one would expect an information processing approach to apply to their work. What needs to be examined is whether or not, as Winograd and Flores suggest, this new discourse leads to changes in the world the students construct.

Examples of student responses to the survey are contained in Appendix Two.

Surprises

My information processing expectations had been subverted. The model of Mind shared by many young people was multi-faceted and richly diverse. It did accept the information processing paradigm, but there was much more to their concepts than that.

One evening I was discussing my dilemma with a colleague. Whilst I outlined my findings and tried to organise them into some kind of taxonomy I found myself thinking of the ways in which the students, the cyborgs, had worked. All of the aspects of Mind that the students had detailed, and the eclectic working patterns they adopted appeared to form part of a pattern.

I found myself thinking of Levi Strauss' concept of bricolage. This was the model that I took forward to the next stage.

9   Towards a new theory of Mind

The surveys of student computer use undertaken over more than five years of the study showed students using Information Technology tools to undertake tasks across the whole of their education. Key Skills has been embedded in the post-16 curriculum and in vocational training. The principles of the Literacy Hour and the Numeracy Hour have moved from the primary school into the secondary school. These Key Skills by any other name are likely to by joined by ICT. When that happens they will form the core curriculum for all students.

Surveys of teacher competence in the use and application of ICT during the same period have highlighted a growing disparity between students and their teachers. Where teaching in ICT takes place much of it is skills-based. It focuses on exercises, which are assessed on the basis of how well the student has fulfilled the expectations of the teacher and the assignment. The outcome is often a set of imperfectly-learned routines with limited transfer possibilities. This is particularly the case where schools have decided to allocate an hour a week to ICT as a taught subject, in order that National Curriculum responsibilities be met. The intention may be that ICT is to be taught as a tool, but because resources are often inadequate students rarely have the opportunity to use it as a tool except in tightly controlled circumstances.

Interviews with students, however, indicate that their starting points for work are what they already know, and what is available for their use. The conventional instructional paradigm holds that the learner is introduced to a new program, practises the skills and then applies them in a relevant task. However, this is not that which students apply to their own Information Technology use.

Tasks which students undertake represent the unknown: they try to solve problems and complete work at the same time. The old paradigm of learning, practice and application has little relevance to tasks which they undertake. The constant updating of hardware and software means that few schools have the resources or the time to ensure that students learn, practise and apply their ICT skills. What is happening is that students apply the programs they have to the task in hand, and try to learn the routines as they go along. The use of the tool becomes shaped by the outcome, and the skills develop through use. The practice becomes one of 'do-it-yourself', in which items are taken 'off the shelf' and used in whatever way the constructor sees fit.

The French term for this is 'bricolage' - whether for a do-it-yourself store, a builders' merchant or the act of constructing an artefact in this way. In 'The Savage Mind' (1962) Levi Strauss used the term 'Bricolage' to describe the way in which the non-literate, non-technical Mind of 'primitive' man responds to the world around him. The process involves a 'science of the concrete' which is carefully and precisely ordered, classified and structured by means of its own logic. The structures are 'made up', and are ad-hoc responses to an environment. They establish homologies and analogies between the ordering of nature and that of society, and 'explain' the world and make it able to be lived in. The bricoleur constructs the 'messages' whereby 'nature' and 'culture' are caused to mirror each other. Levi Strauss saw bricolage as a way in which pre-scientific societies construct a belief system which explained their world.

Papert (1980) used the concept of bricolage in relation to the concept of 'chunking' (Miller, 1956), a process in which knowledge is broken into 'Mind-size bites', which enables new knowledge and understanding to be constructed from it. His thesis was that the use of previously learned strategies - specifically LOGO routines - could be used as a tool by children in concept formation.

Levi Strauss' explanation of bricolage and the bricoleur offers an insight that is, perhaps, more applicable to our students.

> ...a bricoleur is someone who works with his hands and uses devious means compared to those of a craftsman...(he) has nothing else at (his) disposal. ... The bricoleur is adept at performing a large number of diverse tasks...the rules of his game are always to make do with 'whatever is at hand'. (p.17.)

The process used by students, then, is one of working from the specific (the assignment or task that must be completed) to the general (learning from that experience to apply to future experiences). The signs by which they work are those of the Graphical User Interface, with its buttons, toolbars, the ability to undo errors and print preview work in progress. The 'devious means' which they use involve templates and wizards, making do with 'whatever is at hand'. Their work gives an account of their lives in a world where allusion, reference and quotation seem the only possibility.

> We have already noticed the connection between…the activities of the…bricoleur and the modus operandi of the jazz musician. …This art, - an art of signifiers, not signifieds, can be said to be truly modern…
>
> (Hawkes, 1977, p.121.)

If the analogy of 'do-it-yourself' is developed, then one needs to examine the tools and materials that a bricoleur can find to hand.

The toolbox

The toolboxes with which students work can be found at home, amongst their peers, and in educational establishments. The ubiquitous personal computer with a 3.5-inch disk drive can be used to achieve at least part of whatever task is in progress. A collection of floppy disks will store all of the parts that have been fabricated: the artefact will be assembled in whatever space offers the best facilities. A CD-writer extends the range of possibilities, whilst online storage resources can be accessed by students from whatever location for whatever purpose, be it individual or collaborative.

The diversity of information technology provision in educational institutions is a by-product of the speed of technical change and of the continuous consumption predicated by built-in obsolescence. The same pattern can be found amongst individuals: what was state-of-the art six months previously is no longer marketed. The cutting edge of technology slices the market into as many segments as there are owners, many of whom imagined that their purchases would have the same life span as other consumer items such as video recorders or washing machines.

Students learn to use a range of tools in whatever way they can. Old 286 machines can be used to create and edit text and data: a 386 will be used for that, and more. Computers with a 486 processor serve as workhorses, whilst the serious work is done on the newest, fastest machines with the largest memory and the biggest hard drives. Scanners and digital cameras will grab all the images that are needed. Institutional Internet access, with greater bandwidth and faster connection speeds than at home will provide serendipitous information sources.

The tools

> ...the engineer works by means of concepts and the 'bricoleur' by means of signs.
>
> (Levi Strauss, 1962; 1972, p. 20.)

Throughout the research it has been noted that students work with whatever software tools are to hand. These tools range from the basic integrated Works packages installed on educational networks, through those, like Lotus SmartSuite or Corel WordPerfect Suite, which are bundled (for market share) with machines sold into the domestic market, to the latest incarnation of Microsoft's Office. The more enterprising students download freeware or beta versions of programs from the Internet. DTP programs, publishing packages and presentation software are all available, to be picked up and used when they are needed. The CD-ROM cover disks that are given away with computer magazines are passed around if they contain games, programs or useful utilities. Oracle's Think.com links students to world-wide collaborative communities and provides a forum for publishing.

Students work with Wizards in order to short-cut the learning curve. Wizards provide a way in which users can approach a task for the first time and be guided through a range of options. Auto-content and templates provide ideas and suggestions: choices are provided which users can accept or reject at will; preview possibilities and choose the one most appropriate to their needs. They offer a framework for learning in which the learner is in charge.

Success with one piece of work encourages further experimentation: the main skill that is learned is the speed with which things can be learned.

What remains to be done by the student is to knit together all of the work created by these tools. Students learn how to save and import in various file formats. Having done so, they pass that knowledge on to others. Work is copied from one application and pasted into another. All these are done in the teeth of rapidly approaching deadlines: writing, creating and editing are simultaneous. As each part of the edifice is put into place it is saved: if it does not look right, or if the structure topples, then the UNDO command restores the status quo. In this way, numbers of pieces can be tried out, considered and modified before the deadline arrives and the work is submitted. The process is one of intuitive navigation through a series of mid-course corrections. Students have often referred to this as 'tweaking' or 'tinkering'.

The materials

> ...he 'speaks' not only with things...but also through the medium of things: giving an account of his personality and life by the choices he makes between the limited possibilities.
>
> (Levi Strauss, 1962; 1972, p. 21.)

This Do-it-Yourself approach affords equality to all materials. Student-generated text is no more privileged a discourse than text downloaded from the Internet, saved from a CD-ROM or scanned from other text sources. Images taken from clip art collections are modified at will and used in conjunction with others scanned from books, magazines and photographs or grabbed by video capture. The Web is seen as an infinite resource of images and code as well as information. These materials, then, are seemingly endless: the needs of the task, the tools to hand, the knowledge pool and the time available are the only constraints.

The artefacts

An artefact that illustrates the dilemma which this poses to educational institutions was produced in response to a Year 9 Geography assignment which was set at Boston Spa Comprehensive School. This required students to research and write a paper on earthquakes. Responses varied from handwritten explanations drawn from a range of textbooks with appropriate hand-drawn coloured diagrams, through bald summaries of lesson notes, to work resourced from, and produced through, ICT. The most imaginative example of the latter category was produced by a student who utilised diagrams from Encarta entries, saved a sequence of images from the video clips as individual frames and chose text samples to illustrate the process. These were then copied and pasted into a document and presented as his own work. His (original) written contribution was a series of headings and an explanatory commentary.

This assignment elicited a number of responses from teachers. Many thought that the report somehow short-changed the educational process. The student admitted that the report had been completed in half an hour. Many students had spent weeks on their reports, struggling to share library books and produce neat work. Nevertheless, in terms of both cognition and outcome the student with a home PC and Encarta had achieved what the assignment intended.

Presentation software provides enhanced opportunities for students to embed headings and explanatory commentary in a format that uses images and effects to communicate. These postmodern collagistes cut and paste images into the presentation framework and thread their message through the medium. The information is carried both visually and textually.

In an early (1996) example of PowerPoint by a Year 12 GNVQ Business (Advanced) student, images and text were combined to illustrate a talk on employment and the law. As with many such presentations the student incorporated text from the report into the slide show. The result was that effect of the image is minimised. The amount of text meant that the value of the image was more decorative than semiotic. By the following year students were adapting their style to match the presentation. Standard layouts and images from PowerPoint were still used, but the quantity of text had reduced.

Year 11 students in a GCSE Geography project the same year (1997) collaborated to produce a report of their field trip. The majority of the images were drawn from the clip art library, but a map had been scanned and inserted into the presentation. Student annotated the images with points from their study. By the following year students undertaking the same project were thinking in terms of digital cameras and scanners. An increasing number of computers targeted at the consumer market were bundled with these peripherals. Three of the images in their sequence were digitised photographs. The fourth image had been scanned from an existing picture.

As students gained increased access to computers in school and at home, the level of complexity of their work increased. Their slides demonstrated complex editing, with a range of images and techniques incorporated into the final product. When a Geography teacher set homework, one Year 9 student simply inserted images and selected text from the multimedia encyclopaedia Encarta into PowerPoint templates. These were then printed out and used as coursework. In later examples images were downloaded from the Web and incorporated into a presentation templates.

Web pages produced by students used a similar design approach: page design was often based on that produced by others: source code for images and effects copied and pasted into the students' own sites. Indeed, hosts such as GeoCities distribute free utilities to encourage web site construction.

The problems

The post-modern positioning and conditioning of students, accessing, copying and swapping a range of media, extends to the work that they do. They regard the artefact they produce for assessment as their product: they have designed and created it. In essence, it is a post-copyright product. In their world, what are the ethics of ownership? What are intellectual property rights in the Information Age? What is plagiarism?

A presentation made by a Year 12 GNVQ (Intermediate) student to report on his work experience integrated word processing, PagePlus (a DTP program) and stock clip art from PowerPoint. The student also used the Print Screen facility to save screen shots which illustrated the tasks he undertook on work experience. These were then integrated with the rest of his work. The main signifiers on the slides were the images: the text simply supplied the detail. The student had started to move away from a dependency on text. Whilst undertaking work on a database during his work experience the student selected the 'Print Screen' option and saved the image to his floppy disk. On his return to school the image was imported into a DTP program, text superimposed, then copied and pasted into the PowerPoint file.

In an ideal world there would be time, resources and expertise enough to ensure that the educational process empowered all of our students equally. What we see, however, is that in this Information Age, those with access to the economic and cultural capital which computers represent are privileged.

> I got my first computer when I was five. I've had lots since then. I always use them.
>
> (Year 12 GNVQ Student.)

These students envisage any tasks which they are set in terms of the resources and routines which they will use. The proportion of their week in which computers are used is considerably greater than most of their teachers. Apart from access during timetabled lessons, students have access before school, at break, during lunch-times and after school. When they go home to work many of them switch on their computer. (Year 7: 47% Year 10: 62%; Year 12/13: 72%.) It is only to be expected that their proficiency should be more extensive.

When the starting position of many students is compared with that of their teachers it becomes clear that it is critical to develop a range of strategies to cope with the ways in which many school students work. The first imperative is that information seeking and handling skills should be taught as an integral part of the curriculum from the earliest age. The second imperative is that schools and teachers address the issue of those students who do not have access to a home PC. A policy of positive discrimination may be needed. It may be necessary to re-define our expectations of coursework in order that no group of students is disadvantaged: neither those from non-digital households, nor those who are electronic magpies, plucking glittering items from whatever source they find and constructing their artefacts.

A key issue is that students be taught the attribution and ethical use of materials. Plagiarism of a textbook is easier for a teacher to identify than that of a plethora of electronic information. Those students who have CD-ROMs and an Internet connection at home have access to an unlimited source of information which teachers cannot control, or indeed identify.

The progress of these cyborgs from the classroom into higher education inevitably raises questions about the nature of authenticity and originality of their work. The issues raised are ones that are of direct concern to teachers. If they are not addressed at an early enough stage in the educational process there may well be two inevitable consequences:

- more ammunition will be handed to those critics of the expansion of higher education, who would argue that true learning is the province of the few, rather than the resource of the many;
- those students whose understanding and use of computers is limited by their lack of access will be further marginalised.

A new (autonomous) way of working?

The process used by students, then, is one of working from the specific (the assignment or task that must be completed) to the general (learning from that experience to apply to future experiences). The signs by which they work are those of the Graphical User Interface, with its buttons, toolbars, the ability to undo and print-preview work in progress. The 'devious means' which they use involve templates and wizards, making do with 'whatever is at hand'. Their work gives an account of their lives in a world where allusion, reference and quotation seem the only possibility. The dominance of a post-modern culture, which resists both privileged readings and traditional narratives, suggests an outlook very different to a Hegelian sense of thesis, antithesis and synthesis.

What do you do when you have to learn and those who should teach you don't know?

The background of many teachers in the past thirty years has been based on the concept of developmental stages in learning (Piaget, 1958). This posits three main stages through which the learner must pass - sensori-motor, concrete and iconic - before anything of significance can be produced. Much of the pedagogical culture of schools (and teacher ideology) is loosely based on a conflation of these stages and 'developmental readiness'. Teacher input, student practice and application (or transfer) are often assumed to be the appropriate model for student learning. The education system itself, with its primary - secondary - tertiary divides, and the ways in which educational resources are allocated, provides the material base for this superstructure.

Learners with access to computers have established a different material base. The speed and capability of machines, with their 'Point and Click' ostensiveness, templates and wizards, have usurped their teachers' paradigm. Learners practise the skills and concepts whilst applying them: where input or explanation is necessary the task will be suspended. The Help facility, a magazine article or a conversation with a friend should resolve the problem. Only rarely will the student consult the user manual.

To the thesis of Stages of Learning there is now an antithesis: There Are No Mistakes. The alterations in the task are part of the learning. Students use Edit: Undo; Edit: Clear or Exit: Don't Save. The process is auto-didactic.

The material base of computer access supports a superstructure with its twin pillars of apparent wisdom. The first assumption on the part of many students is that "the answer is out there": that information access through the use of CD-ROMs and the Internet, and information handling through cutting and pasting and downloading, will somehow lead to knowledge and understanding. The second assumption is that the most important aspect of a piece of work is its originality in creative terms. The creation of artefacts is a process of self-expression; the do-it-yourself of bricoleurs.

The synthesis must be that learning is seen as experiential, observational and a semiotic experience. The question of content, contentious when what has been done is not worth learning, must not be subverted by electronic form.

Concern over the subversion of content by electronic form has been identified as 'data dandyism' (Lovink 1995). He describes those who are "...concerned with...the accumulation of as many immaterial ornaments as possible...", where digital style triumphs over substance. The ornaments are a reflection of both technical skill, in that the 'data dandy' demonstrates superior competence, and technical sophistication, in that the user possesses the latest, most powerful (and most expensive) hardware, software and peripherals. The sub-text is that the user has sufficient time to devote to the acquisition of such skills. This demonstration of social worth through cyber semiotics updates the concept of fashion and conspicuous consumption (Veblen, 1899).

Or is the substance inseparable from the style?

> ...a bricoleur is someone who works with his hands and uses devious means compared to those of a craftsman...(he) has nothing else at (his) disposal. ... The bricoleur is adept at performing a large number of diverse tasks...the rules of his game are always to make do with 'whatever is at hand'.
> ...the engineer works by means of concepts and the 'bricoleur' by means of signs.
> ...he 'speaks' not only with things...but also through the medium of things: giving an account of his personality and life by the choices he makes between the limited possibilities.
>
> (Levi Strauss.)

> We have already noticed the connection between...the activities of the...bricoleur and the modus operandi of the jazz musician. ...This art, - an art of signifiers, not signifieds, can be said to be truly modern...
>
> (Hawkes.)

Our post-modern bricoleurs in cyberspace

Do-It-Yourself for cyborgs

> *Use the bits of Information and Communications Technologies to construct metaphors for who you think you may be.*
>
> *Be a Bricoleur of the Future, for the Future.*

10 Why can't teachers do IT? Cognitive dissonance

Problems teachers face with ICT

Teachers have four major problems with which to contend when attempting to master the application, content and concepts of Information and Communication Technology. These are the problems of ownership; time; access (and equality) and learning patterns unsuited to ICT.

Ownership

Surveys undertaken for this research showed fewer than 60% of teachers had access to a home computer. Of those who did, there was a variety of types and operating systems that reflected provision in their schools. Acorn computers were the dominant system for many schools in Leeds LEA, and this was reflected in patterns of teacher ownership. The prevalence of word processing as the main task to which teachers put computers means that there was not necessarily an imperative to upgrade machines regularly in order to accommodate the latest programs. Only in the last few years, with the advent of PC as consumer package, did 'PC' become synonymous with 'computer' for teachers.

The net result of this was that in many cases teachers found that they had a make of machine and an operating system which was not the same as their students. The processes with which they as individuals were most comfortable were (and are) reflected in their classroom applications, which tend to be structured in curriculum terms. The readiness to treat computers as short-life consumer items rather than consumer durables, and to constantly upgrade hardware and software, was not as apparent with teachers as with their students.

The cost of new machines as a percentage of teachers' disposable income was an additional disincentive for change. Only with the introduction of the Computers for Teachers scheme, where teachers were able to claim a subsidy from the DfEE against the purchase of a computer, was there a financial incentive for teachers to purchase a high-specification machine with Internet access.

Time

One of the central issues confronting teachers is the amount of time which it takes to master new routines and programs before they feel a level of competence which enables their integration into classroom routines. In part there is a direct correlation between this problem and that of ownership. Unless teachers have direct access to the latest technology, and can use this in their daily routines, then they will be at a marked disadvantage compared with students who use machines in a variety of applications, for a variety of purposes, throughout the school day as well as at home.

There are very few teachers who are privileged to have a computer for their personal use at work: those who are in that fortunate position use it for a fraction of their working day. Few schools have been organised and resourced in such a way that ICT is integrated into the physical and curricular fabric of the school. As a result, the appreciation of the ways in which ICT can be used, and an understanding of the ways in which it can be learned, are of necessity limited. Workers in industries other than education who have this awareness pass it on to their children. Given these circumstances, it is not only difficult for teachers to bridge the gap, but difficult for many to perceive that the gap exists.

Access and equality

The introduction of a consumer technology that impacts on the educational process raises the issue of equality: those students who have access to a computer at home are often at an advantage over those who are reliant on machines at school. This is particularly the case for students who produce coursework for examination subjects. The amount of time which can be spent on work by students with computers at home, and the use of tools to remove surface errors, very often leads to higher examination grades than for those without. Teachers' views cited in the section 'What teachers think about IT' reflect that.

The unease which this generates leads many teachers to wonder about the disparity between schools: the provision which some schools can offer their students is considerably greater than others. When differentials are compounded by a perception of social inequality there is an understandable reluctance on the part of some to include within compulsory education a technology which embodies this. The charge of Luddism directed at such teachers may appear to be true: they are not, however, protecting their privileged position, but rather see themselves as defending the less privileged. If part of the curriculum can be maintained as an ICT-free zone, then many people feel that those with limited access to such resources are less likely to be disadvantaged.

How do teachers learn?

Teachers learn in ways that they know are successful. They have reached their position because they were successful at the type of learning which education demanded. In addition they bring to the task of learning a model of learning which they use in their work. Teachers have found that success within the education system is through listening; taking notes; practising and using reference books: these steps are repeated, until they feel that learning has taken place. They can then apply the learning to a specific task. The process is empirical: it involves the reduction of wholes to their constituent parts as the ultimate building blocks of knowledge.

Knowledge and truth are constructed from individual terms and propositions, which can then be fitted together as scaffolding, to support concepts. These isolated terms and propositions can also be learned by the students, assessed by their teachers, verified by the education hierarchy and published in league tables.

Cultural capital

These four factors - ownership; time; access and equality and learning patterns unsuited to ICT - have inhibited the integration of ICT into classrooms. Teachers, unlike many of the families of young people in this survey, do not have access to a supply of surplus machines which they can purchase for a nominal cost. These factors contribute to teachers' failure to acquire the cultural capital which many of their students possess. A consequence of this is that issues such as plagiarism, copyright, ownership and attribution are not part of many teachers' concerns. Collaborative student work, on the other hand, is often seen in negative terms, since the school-based assessment demands the work of an individual. This is in stark contrast to the way in which learning and work is perceived in industry.

How do students learn?

Students who use computers at school and at home learn to use them by themselves. In order to do this they use a number of strategies. They watch – either what happens on the screen or other students at work. They learn how to utilize the machine because they have tasks to complete: without the machine they couldn't do the tasks. They learn because they can switch from one screen to another, one program to another, in the same way as they can zap from channel to channel on television with a remote control.

Students wander around whilst they are trying to work out a resolution to a problem, or the most appropriate way to accomplish a task. Things are left undone, half finished, whilst they use the ALT/TAB keys to switch between programs. They go for Best Fit in order to make applications work together, data integrate and meet their deadlines. The learning patterns they are developing are not those of their teachers, but they work..

The more they use these strategies with work they have to do, the more they are likely to apply them to situations in which their teachers have predicated the learning on more conventional patterns. Comments from students during the surveys indicated the ways in which this was the case, and the way in which many students felt that the site of learning (as well as production) was at home, in front of 'their' computer.

This is the fundamental problem, which must be addressed by both teachers and the education system. If school is not seen as the principal site of learning work for the majority of students, then what is it for?

A new paradigm for learning: bricoleurs in cyberspace

The new learning patterns that have developed as a result of students utilising computers incorporate ostensiveness, cyber-semiotics, a sense of making-do, allusion, reference and quotation. Their working methods are approximate: they tinker, tweak, learn from their mistakes and steer whatever path is necessary to reach their objective.

Conclusions?

The final survey carried out at Boston Spa Comprehensive School, in 1999, showed that 81% of students had access to a PC at home. Latest industry figures suggest that more than 70% of households in the United Kingdom with school-age children own a PC.

If these children were dependent upon institutionalised learning in order to use the computers, then they'd either be working out LOGO routines, trying to cheat their way through CAL or CALL programs, following sequenced exercises to practice Office routines, or sitting looking bored whilst somebody else sat at the keyboard and told them what was happening.

But they are not. They are using the things. And they learned how to do it. The challenge for teachers and educational institutions is to understand HOW they learned. Then accepted interpretations of learning patters and teaching routines can be mapped onto these.

The problem is that our conventional scales against which we can measure these are calibrated for the education system.

Surprises

During the course of this research my praxis, my understanding and concepts were changed. They were changed by what I discovered; by what I learned from the students; by using the technology. As a teacher, however, I often found myself looking in the wrong direction, for the wrong things. It was only later that I saw what had gone on.

11   The autonomous learner?

...free to explore, to create and to feel ...

(Clynes and Kline.)

Connections

Observations of young people at work with computers, conversations with them and the assessment and analysis of their coursework led me to believe that a fundamental shift had taken place in their approach to work. They no longer saw the structured, linear approach that characterised their lessons as appropriate to them. Further, their conceptualisations of Mind, and the ways in which they perceived the thinking process, suggested that this method of work might not be as ad-hoc as many of us had thought.

Conventions

This research identified a working style used by students analogous to that described as 'bricolage' by Levi-Strauss. This method of working, 'pre-scientific' in Levi-Strauss' view, may well be one that has been intuitive to young people before being supplanted by the systematic, structured method of the education system.

This structured and sequential model, devised, administered and validated by adults, has traditionally imposed itself on that of children. Within this system, success has been measured by the way in which learners have matched those patterns expected by their teachers: adults. In order to succeed, therefore, the learners have had to adopt the systems and patterns expected of them. National Curriculum testing, GCSE and the plethora of post-16 examinations are all dependent upon students generating the outcomes expected by examiners.

Assumptions

The 'developmental folk myth' which informs many teachers' praxis, based upon the popularisation of Piagetian theory, expects learners to pass through a series of stages, each predicating its successor. This praxis contains two pillars of received wisdom: learner readiness, and stage competence. What this means for students is that, first, they are not expected to be able to cope with concepts and applications which have been determined to lie outside the bounds of their developmental stage: second, that each stage needs to be consolidated by practice.

Much of Piaget's research took as its focus the growth of mathematical and scientific concepts. Children's ability to understand the tasks which they were set, and to explain them in appropriate terms, was taken as a demonstration of their competence: the language encoded the 'scientific' expectations imposed on the children. The methodology and findings have been questioned by a number of researchers (Donaldson, 1978; Gardner, 1983, 1993; Seigel and Brainerd, 1978) but the original thesis still retains its power over pedagogy, teacher attitudes and the curriculum for schools in this country.

Broad stages of learning

The broad stages of the learning paradigm can be summarised as those of learning about; practising and applying. The model is very much one of an apprenticeship, with the teacher (and adult) in the role of the master and controller, who is also the assessor of success and competence. The ultimate arbiter and guarantor of success is the state, through its networks of control over schools, examination boards and universities.

The content and form of learning is therefore both constructed and legitimated in academic and social terms. The application of league tables as an apparently neutral scale against which success and failure can be measured is used for the whole of the education systems, whether state or independent, nursery school or Oxbridge college. The debate over standards is one which is externally imposed on the system, with the students as learners constantly scrutinised to determine whether or not their successes are real or the product of an academic inflation that results in a devaluation of the currency. Concurrent with this is the constant scrutiny of the curriculum, to determine whether the cultural capital upon which the students are presuming to trade is genuine or counterfeit, and whether or not Media Studies is as 'real' a subject as Physics and Mathematics.

New realities

Students use their computers as far more than electronic typewriters. The practice of bricolage observed among, and described by, so many students during the course of this study is made possible because of the infinitely flexible tools of hardware and software which they use. These tools become more powerful with each update of existing software and the addition of new. Students seek out downloads of new software in its beta testing format, accepting the instability and glitches built into the system in order that they can try new possibilities. Each addition to their toolbox calls upon new working strategies and new ways in which to learn how to make things work together.

New ways of learning

These cyber-bricoleurs constitute a new knowledge community. Its members are all those who use ICT in innovative ways: adult mentors from work placements; teachers whom they feel are in touch with the latest developments; email correspondents but, most of all, other students. The knowledge pool consists of 'know-how', which constantly renews itself: it is practice, which creates new ways of doing things. It is precisely because of this constant renewal that the knowledge community is separate from that of most teachers.

The knowledge that is constructed is not achieved through linear, sequenced steps. Indeed, it is not achieved by 'chunking' in its accepted sense, since chunking is a concept based on pre-determined structures and stages. Instead, the knowledge is constructed in terms of language, the iconic representation of the Graphical User Interface and the outcomes which they produce. This knowledge construction is dynamic. Students tinker, tweak and work towards the final artefact which in its construction will define the knowledge, both for the student auteur and others of the peer group.

The content and form of the learning are thus inscribed within the artefacts produced: knowledge becomes tangible. If there is no artefact produced then there is no knowledge. Knowledge and outcome are synonymous. These students, cyber-bricoleurs, have become digital auteurs. Where film theory described the auteur as creating an entire conception with celluloid, or transforming a given script by imposing personal pre-occupations and continuing themes through the visual artefact, so these students work with their 'tools at hand' to transform the scripts handed to them by their teachers. The creations of these auteurs serve as metaphors for education. They have become self-referencing semiotic objects, both signifiers and signified.

Life-long learning and implications for schools

Students who use ICT as an integral part of their work develop learning strategies of their own. What these strategies have in common is that they build forward, towards an outcome, rather than building upon established blocks. Where routines from previous learning can be made to work they will be incorporated: where not, new ones will be developed. Students move from the specific to the general, and back again. Content is subordinate to, and subsumed within, structure.

A clash of learning styles

These strategies put them at variance with the majority of their teachers, whose approach to learning, content and outcomes tends to be fixed. Their expectations for the stages through which their students should pass and the outcomes which should be demonstrated are predicated on a empirical framework, constructed from their own professional education, experience and an occasional space for reflection. The likelihood of this matching that of their students is slight.

Structural inequalities

If there is a disjunction between teachers and the way in which these bricoleurs work and learn, then there is also one between these students and those who have limited access to ICT.   Students whose access to ICT is limited therefore do not work or learn in this way, but have to accommodate themselves to the institutional paradigm. The disjunction is encoded in the concepts attached to work and the outcomes it produces. It is encoded in the expectations which each group brings to work.   Most of all, it is encoded in the sense of autonomy which the bricoleurs possess, which their teachers do not expect and which other students may not feel.

The means of production

The result is a structural inequality: of productive capital; of cultural capital and of symbolic capital. The surveys have identified the increase in ownership of the technology. With this has come independence. Initially this was independence from the constraints of time and resources associated with school. This developed to independence from the limitations of software applications, as students appropriated programs from CD-ROMS provided by magazine and from software downloaded from the Internet. When this is combined with access to the seemingly unlimited information of CD-ROM and Internet sources the result is freedom from institutional constraints. The student in school has moved from the position of a subject following prescribed sequences of activities, to that of creative entrepreneur carrying out commissions.

ICT is still regarded by many in education as an innovative technology. For most students, on the other hand, it has diffused into their lives. The gains which this produces not only lead to the increase in productivity that has been noted, but to a change in the way in which the production process is viewed: beliefs, values and praxis have changed.

Cultural capital

This ownership of the means of production leads to the accretion of cultural capital. The beliefs, value systems and production of artefacts shared by the practitioners are based upon a pool of knowledge and practice that is rapidly moving away from the mainstream of educational praxis. The modernist paradigm of a transparent technology, of structured systems, analysis and logical progression has been replaced by one of opacity, in which surface, simulation and 'play' are dominating.

The classroom cyborgs operate within this new domain. Their teachers do not.

Our cyborgs are establishing what Jameson (1991) terms a new domain of cognitive mapping, in which the individual subject establishes its own place in a global system. Not only does this need no legitimation from the school system, but the system finds its claims to legitimation weakened the further apart the two views move.

Symbolic capital

Computers present us with an opaque technology. In other words, the process is no longer apparent when they are used. When computer users had to enter a string of commands to activate a program or activity there was an apparent connection between what was done and what happened. If the user made a mistake, then either nothing, or the wrong thing happened. The point and click ostensiveness of the Graphical User Interface removes the transparency.

The icons and symbols of the Graphical User Interface merge with the icons of the web. The latest manifestation of the Windows operating system claims 'seamless' integration with the web. Folders containing our documents, programs and online information sources all appear as one on the screen. Each time the user connects online there is the opportunity to update: what is new is what is now. In an auto-iterative system there is only the new, and there is no shock. In a virtual world the chief virtue is to read the simulations and build them into new forms. The modernist approach of systems, forms and control has no value in virtuality. The symbolic capital is in the hands of those who navigate the screens, manipulate the representations and who interpret the readings.

Differentials: of work and reward

Post-industrial economies such as the United Kingdom have undergone a significant shift in the structure of the workforce and the distribution of wealth. A definitive analysis may only be possible with the benefit of considerable historical hindsight, since many of the observed trends may well be of less significance than we suppose. In the opening of the new millennium there is furious debate about the worth and value of the information industries, compared with what are deemed to be 'real' industries. What is incontrovertible, however, is the correlation between flexibility, innovation, transferable skills and reward.

We can apply the analogy of the economy to work within schools, and the rewards attached to it. Whilst the terms primary, secondary and tertiary have their own connotations within education a different interpretation can be applied.

Work of a primary nature is limited to a system of decoding texts, information and knowledge, which results in the production of basic answers.

This approach to learning is teacher-controlled. Students who work in this way require constant input. Their productive output is directly related to this, and as such may easily be modified, corrected and assessed by their teachers. The curriculum within which they work is dominant. This is the conventional view of the educational process, reflected in approaches to the curriculum.

Secondary production involves the re-working and sequencing of the primary parts. The teachers define both the input and acceptable forms of output. The decoded elements are interpreted.

The secondary stage of educational production is also curriculum-based and dependent upon plans, schemes of work and quality control. It is subject to the constant monitoring and scrutiny which produces quantifiable performance statistics and league tables. The modernist concept of 'value-added' is important at this stage of production. The school plant and teacher workforce are measured by the way in which they can improve the raw material of students by the application of National Curriculum and examination syllabus input.

In the tertiary stage we observe the application of texts, information and knowledge. These elements are capable of continual synthesis. The production process involves continuous innovation and syncretic thinking.

The students who form this group work as auteurs. They determine their own references and standards, whilst working with the given educational script. Their initial critics are students like themselves. These are the students engaging in the process of bricolage. What is significant is that, whilst the stage of secondary production is built on the primary base, there is no necessity for the tertiary superstructure to be a sequential development of the earlier stages. The material base for this stage is that of the productive capital that has already been described.

The rewards that may be earned by the first two stages of knowledge production are clearly understood by teachers, assessors and examiners within education, and bestowed by them. They form part of an established value system. The knowledge workers of the tertiary stage create their own values. Earlier measuring systems can no longer apply.

The nature of education

One of the recurrent themes of the education debates of the past forty years has been that of content against process. The introduction of the National Curriculum, with what many teachers see as a prescriptive syllabus and a mandatory content, would suggest that learner-centred education, with the student constructing her own knowledge, has been relegated to the footnotes of state education. At first sight it may appear as if the cyborgs of the tertiary sector of educational production are the standard-bearers of post-modern relativist process. Their praxis, however, is one that constructs knowledge: the working heuristic of discovery (Bruner, 1974). They take for granted the scripts within which they work. What they produce is a result of their discovery of the ways in which the information given and found, the tools to hand and the time available can be transmuted into their creation. The artefact is the manifestation of their conceptual development.

What curricular requirements, productive capital and their creation of knowledge lack is the ethical base which a post-modern hermeneutics requires. In a world where information sources are available to anyone with online access there is an imperative for students to be taught the need for a system of citations and attributions, that knowledge and information are not simply commodities to be appropriated at will. In earlier stages of the education process students work with known information and sources, which their teachers control and recognise. The challenge for the teachers of these post-modern auto-epistemologists is to establish an ethical framework within which the new praxis can be located. Research for the Teacher Training Agency on teachers as innovators would appear to confirm this (Preston, Cox and Cox, 2000).

The autonomous learner

In a traditional approach to education teachers have motivated their students; students have motivated themselves to meet targets set by either their teachers or the system itself. The motivation for learning is therefore contained within and supported by the system. The new approach requires learners to be self-motivated. Rewards have to be intrinsic, rather than extrinsic. The new way of working, however, seeks to bring with it the approval of the peer group, who comment on the production values contained within the work. (This factor was recognised in early research into students and computers. (Somekh, 1986, in: Schostak, 1988).) What is now necessary is for teachers to provide clear performance criteria and evidence indicators for students' work. Whilst the traditional roles of a teacher will remain, those of advocate, mentor and verifier will need to be added.

The role of advocate will be two-fold: first, as advocate for the subject material and the discipline of which it is a part; second, as advocate for the long-term interests of the student. This will require an understanding of their working practices, neither being dazzled by the skills which they possess (the 'data dandies'), nor complaining about their lack of a traditional approach (Somekh and Davis, 1997).

A partnership of learning

The role of mentor will require a fundamental shift in the traditional relationship between student and teacher. That relationship had traditionally been predicated on the assumption that the teacher and the school would provide the information which the student required. Where that is no longer the case the teacher needs to provide guidance for the student through the task to be done, using pedagogical skills to suggest a range of possibilities to the student and leave open the specific outcomes.

The teacher will then be able to verify whether or not the student has achieved the objectives specified in the performance criteria and generated the relevant evidence indicators. Bruner's working heuristic of discovery will be created in the partnership of teacher, student and computer. For Life Long Learning to succeed there must be a partnership, and there must be a working heuristic of discovery. Without those two factors there will be training, rather than learning. The focus will be utilitarian and specifically focused. The shape and outcomes will be defined by others. The disjunction which has been identified, between learners who are establishing their autonomy and an educational approach that leans towards the prescriptive, it is the prescriptive that is likely to increase.

12 Methodology: Reflections

Intentions

The first intention of this study was to determine the levels of computer ownership in school, track the changes over time, compare these levels with those of teachers, and to examine the uses that were being made of the computers themselves.

The second intention was to examine the ways in which the use of a new tool changed the ways in which the users operated.

The third intention was to examine whether the use of this new tool would change the way in which the users thought.

Presenting the data

I concluded that the most effective way to present information about levels of ownership was to convert the data into percentages. What was required was a picture of the levels within each tutor group and year group, and the school as a whole. The figures for tutor groups within a year proved invaluable for curricular analysis. It was possible to identify tutor groups with a lower level of computer use within school, and to examine the reasons for that. In many cases it was possible to compensate by reorganizing the timetable to provide ICT literate teachers, or make additional IT facilities available. Tutor groups that showed a lower level of home access than others were provided with additional basic skills as part of the tutorial programme.

To this end, then, the conversion of data that was used proved effective in providing snapshots of ownership. This picture was transferred to other parts of the curriculum and used as a management tool by team leaders.

Reliability

The reliability of this as a presentation technique was dependant upon the collection being systematic. Collections took place within one week in each year, during the spring term. Some data sets were collected outside this period: staff absence, problems with school buses and unforeseen occurrences all played their part in disturbing the schedule. In the main, however, the surveys were completed by the majority of students who were in tutor time on the morning their group was surveyed. The average was 70% of the school population of 1800 for the five-year period during which data was collected.

The process proved less reliable when the same survey was carried out at City Comprehensive School. Class sets were less than complete; responses from students were less detailed. The biggest limitation, however, was that the data collection took place in December. A number of students commented that they expected to receive a PC for Christmas. Had the survey taken place in February the ownership levels may well have been higher.

External factors

The factor that may have made the biggest difference did not form part of the survey: parental occupation. The type of work, and the environment in which it is carried out, is of possibly more significance than the level of pay. The transfer of information technology from the workplace to the home has already been commented on. During 1995-7 the factor that had the biggest impact on access to computers was the purchase of old machines from work (for a nominal sum) for use at home. It was these Windows-based PCs that steered the shift from games machine to work machines for many students.

By 1997 multimedia computers had become consumer goods. Prices were quoted inclusive of Value Added Tax. They were sold as packages, with printers, scanners, modems and programs bundled together. Many of the programs were pre-installed. Newspaper advertisements targeted home users, with emphasis being placed upon the young. The implication was that all one had to do was remove the machine from the packaging, plug it into a power source and one could take off into the digital world. Easy credit was a prominent part of the advertising. By 1999 the major supermarkets were selling computer packages like any other commodity on their shelves.

Affective responses

As changes in computer access and ownership became readily apparent the focus of investigation shifted from quantitative aspects to qualitative, as affective factors formed a greater part of student response. It was during this period that students were surveyed to determine their responses to issues of computers, coursework and marks; ways in which they worked with computers; how they thought the Mind worked, and what it was; how they learned. Students were initially asked for written responses, either in tutor time or in a timetabled lesson. The majority of these sessions took place at the end of the summer term, when there was space within the timetable. It is for this reason that the samples are smaller: Years 11 and 13 were on study leave.

Students were also observed whilst they were working, either in classrooms or during lunchtime sessions. This was followed by discussion.

Uses and gratifications theory

The method of classifying data which I used, adapted from McQuail's Uses and Gratifications typology, was only used for the first data collection. Subsequent surveys generated most of the same reasons for using computers: It was felt that, since the initial classification provided a picture to inform the study, further analysis of the qualitative data using this framework would yield little that was new.

Part of the problem may well lie in the typology itself. The majority of student responses fell in the category of Personal Identity. It has been said that the concentration of responses in this category renders it invalid. However, since students cited other reasons for using computers as well as the Personal Identity category, it is felt that the link between the tool of the computer and the personal identity of the user is a significant one.

Computers, uses and gratifications: a justification

The criticisms of Uses and Gratifications theory were raised in the opening chapters. In brief, they are that it is too individualistic, that it accepts the uses at face value without interrogating them, that there is no theoretical grounding, that it does no more than collate personal preferences and that it is essentially consumerist, are not directly applicable in this context. The very strong Personal Identity theme corresponds to the work that students are producing with computers, the 'This is me!' factor.

What the framework provided was a tool with which the data could be classified. In that, it more than served its purpose.

13   Conclusion

The hypothesis that framed my study was that of Winograd and Flores (1988).

> As the use of a new technology changes human practices, our ways of speaking about that technology change our language and our understanding. This new way of speaking in turn creates changes in the world we construct.

My initial assumption was that the changes that I would identify in the ways in which young people used the technology, and the changes it produced in their understanding, would relate to their ability to handle, present and process data.

The surveys I conducted for the first three years of this research investigated the material conditions of computer ownership, the understanding of computers which the young people possessed, and the uses to which they were put. During the first survey the definition of 'computer' was broad enough to include a number of machines that were used for games, although the owners were under no illusions as to their use. It was the technology to which the label 'computer' was applied, rather than the application. Other students identified older machines as suitable for practice in programming. The consensus among students at the school, however, was that a 'real' computer was one which contained an Intel processor and used a version of the Windows operating system. This perception was one that had been formed outside school, the dominant influence of which was the environment of work and employment.

What also emerged during the early surveys was the clear distinction made by students as to the way in which computers were used at school and the ways in which they were used at home, even though the work was being produced for school. It was clear that students regarded their systems as an extension of themselves and their personality: the ways in which they used the machines constituted an act of creation.

Very few of these students had received specific teaching in ICT at school: what teacher input there had been had been related to how to use programs on the school network and how to apply these to specific curriculum tasks. In other words, these students had learned how to use the systems themselves. As the proportion of students with access to a computer at home increased so did the number and types of programs they used. CD-ROMS and disks containing applications were regarded as common property: students would install a program, try it out and if useful keep it; if not, delete it. Their relationship with their computers is dynamic. They are in a process of continual learning which they control. By contrast, their relationship with school systems is restricted and static.

The changes in the world these students constructed have been ones of cognition and learning. Computers act as a vehicle for the combination of motor skills, manipulation, language and symbolic manipulation, through practical activities. These activities can range from the installation of programs, through playing games in virtual environments to undertaking a multiplicity of tasks for coursework. The software they use predicates a greater range of possibilities, as the activities for which it is used become more complex.

My initial supposition was that the rule-governed nature of software would produce a systematic approach to tasks that involved data handling and its presentation. That does not appear to have been the case. It is, rather, the plasticity of software and the GUI environment that has presented students with the ability to innovate. It is the ease of experimentation that this offers that liberates the bricoleur within individuals.

The point-and-click environment which students utilise reinforces the power of ostensiveness, the operation of pointing, which reinforces learning through representation by imagery and perceptual organisation. The images are the translation into visual form of prior linguistic and mathematical rendering: students perceive and use the icon as an entity in its own right. This is the 'virtual reality' - not the theoretical underpinning of which it is the iconic representation. The spatio-qualitative qualities and properties of the events which the icons on the screen invoke are subsumed by the act of creation and the object that is created.

The concepts of Mind which the students form are those associated with creativity and originality. These construct the individual's sense of identity. It is a learned construct. For the first time learners have a machine for learning that is powerful, interactive, flexible and personalised. The changes suggested by Winograd and Flores are a product of this, but they are continual changes, a dynamic, the outline of which is only starting to emerge. They have produced an independence in the learners who use computers which is increasingly at variance with institutional expectations of learning, and the relationship between school students and the institution.

For these students, knowledge is in the constructive process: it is concerned with the making of ideas, rather than in finding them to solve a pre-determined problem. In cognitive terms it produces second order cognitive knowledge, which enables students to work things out for themselves and to interpret new structures, rather than first-order tasks, which tend to be teacher-directed (Stevenson, 1998).

Indeed, much research literature is still focused on the institutional perspective. Concern is raised over the effects of multimedia when used in an instructional context: the assumption is that there is an inherent contradiction between the learning styles associated with multimedia and the Internet and the educational process (Salomon, G. 1998). The critique is extended to ICT in American education, and the conclusion reached is that it has produced negative effects (Oppenheimer, 1997). Seymour Papert (1996), on the other hand, approached the subject from the opposite perspective: bottom-up, rather than top-down. His chosen analogy is horticultural: "Give everybody a computer, and then here and there more and more people will find interesting things to do with those computers and new ideas will spontaneously grow."

The model of the education system, based on hierarchical, industrial, modernist assumptions, is one that at present sits uneasily with its subjects. They control their technology: the productive capital. They create their cultural capital. They share a symbolic capital common to those who live in the post-industrial, post-modern digital virtual world.

The challenge for teachers in the classroom is that of presenting the curriculum and the learning process in ways which will enable all to succeed. Those whose intellect and learning style is shaped by their ICT environment must be taught the disciplines of information handling and attribution. Those who are dependent on school-based resources must be provided with an environment in which intellect can be enriched.

The challenge for society and institutions is to incorporate this new reality into their pedagogy and epistemology and ensure that all can benefit from it. If the challenge is not met the structural and cognitive inequalities that will result will impoverish us all.

Reflections

A significant number of students expect to do most of their work at home, rather than at school.

Many students regard the knowledge of how to do things as more important than subject knowledge.

Their computers are vehicles for learning: the routes they use to learn are not those found in most classrooms.

The computer has become the integrating focus for the verbal-linguistic; logical-mathematical; visual-spatial and bodily-kinesthetic intelligences described by Gardner. All these combine in the process of learning for young people.

When knowledge is constructed by the students the teacher finds it very difficult to be a gatekeeper.

New routes, new roles

The research has explored a number of problematic areas in the use of computers by young people. There is no easy solution to their resolution: indeed, we may be trying to solve tomorrow's problems with yesterday's concepts. What follows is an outline of areas for further investigation and work.

Work at home

Many students have moved the site of production from school to home, because that is where their computers are. Their perception is that such work is more highly rewarded by their teachers. They also find it more 'fun'. This generates two additional problems: students without a PC at home may well be disadvantaged further and the nature of work and behaviour in the classroom changes. Teachers find themselves managing groups of young people who do not expect to produce work in the classroom. Where much of the time in secondary school classrooms is devoted to tasks which reinforce learning the perception of both students and teachers must change. The construction of 'work', and its relation to learning, marking and assessment will require some adjustment.

Tools at home

The tools available to many young people: multimedia encyclopedias and reference works on CD-ROM, scanners and cameras for manipulating images and Internet access, call into question the nature of knowledge and how we assess it. Where there is a growing perception that knowledge is inscribed within the artefact students must be taught the skills of information handling and the associated ethics, particularly those related to plagiarism.

School a PC free zone?

School budgeting problems, resourcing issues, concerns over equality and a shortage of suitably skilled and motivated staff could lead some to imagine that the solution is to return to the classrooms of yesterday. If students are accessing information and learning autonomously at home, forming their own intelligence communities, then one role for schools may be to focus on issues other than those involved with ICT. Given the status of ICT within the National Curriculum, the National Grid for Learning, the Virtual Teachers' Centre, and government initiatives to empower young people through 'computer literacy' this is not likely to be an option.

Integrate ICT possibilities into curriculum

The alternative is to integrate ICT within the curriculum. Display technologies, such as those of interactive whiteboards, the use of intranets and the Internet, the falling price of palmtop computers and the development of the National Grid for Learning all suggest that the technology is available if the will to use and integrate it is there.

PC to follow TV?

During the course of this study the PC has become ubiquitous among students at the school. The convergence of computers, Internet, multimedia, television and telecoms may well mean that our current concerns are a passing phase. In the same way in which television and video is used for teaching without having to be taught, we may find that ICT and computers become so embedded within our praxis that they are no longer an issue.

The emergence of WAP mobile telephony, the use of hand-held computers and Internet access through digital television are all indicators of the pervasive nature of ICT. Digital television web access, with bundled office utilities, may make online learning a reality for much of the population. The membership of online learning communities with global links, such as Oracle's Think.com, may help to reduce the digital divide.

Whilst this may be true for developed economies, the Less Developed Economies that contain most of the world's children have little chance of providing their young people with these opportunities. An understanding of this should form part of the ethical responsibilities which our students must assume. As they take a more active role in society it is to be hoped that they are able to contribute to the global economy for the benefit of all its citizens, rather than simply as beneficiaries of low consumer prices for the computer equipment they use.

14 Personal epilogue

Towards the end of his degree course my youngest son telephoned and asked if he could use my computer to produce his dissertation. When he arrived it became apparent that he intended to write the dissertation, rather than simply transcribe it. For a number of years he had been surrounded by computers at home, but the limited exposure to school Acorn computers had produced an aversion that had lasted until that moment. I gave him a brief introduction to Microsoft Word and Windows 95.

His dissertation had to be bound and submitted by that Friday.

"Now's the time." he said. He's a jazz musician. He thinks you can improvise everything.

Whilst we were at work he decided he couldn't cope with my machine and so used his mother's. He spent some time staring at the C-prompt, made a few phone calls and started work. He seemed satisfied with his progress until the following day, when he couldn't find his work. He was reduced to writing notes with a pen and paper. He didn't understand the concept of files and directory structures.

By the third day, however, he was making progress. By the fourth day he'd worked out the layout, inserted footnotes and references and completed it. A number of years' ineffective teaching and failed learning at school had been transcended within a few days, simply because the task had to be completed.

When the words 'education' and 'learning' are used the assumption is that the transactions are mediated through the teacher to the learner. That's certainly true in a structural sense, and I suppose that fact that we earn our living in the industry causes us to invest it with a certain significance. But learning doesn't have to have anything to do with the education system: it's just that education has hi-jacked the whole process, so that learning can only be legitimated through the educational structures - and only those structures that have been invested with status.

In the words of John Holt, "If schools had to teach kids to speak we'd have a lot of dumb kids …".

To paraphrase William Burroughs, any individual who can switch on - and switch off - a computer has control over their own learning. Add the Web to that, with email and web publishing facilities, and your circle is complete. What we have is a pattern of learning that is controlled by the learner.

The learning is determined by need; by interest. Successful patterns of past learning predicate new patterns: one connection leads to another.

The issue is not one of content, but of learning. Not what, but how. If the learning is not successful, then the machine or the program won't work. If you can't read and understand the instructions you've either had it, you guess or make a few calls. A flashing cursor, a ticking clock and approaching deadline are neutral. There's no such thing as failure: either something works, or it doesn't: if it doesn't you try something else.

At the end of this research 81% of students surveyed used 'their' PC to do work. Latest industry figures suggested that almost 70% of households with school-age children owned a PC. Once again, I reflect that if they were dependent upon institutionalised learning, then they'd either be working out LOGO routines, trying to cheat their way through CAL or CALL programs, working their way through unrelated office-type tasks, or sitting looking bored whilst somebody else sat at the keyboard and told them what was happening.

But they're not. They're using the things. They learned how to do it. They are using what they have learned to create new learning. That's the challenge. To understand HOW they learned, and map our own interpretation of learning patterns and teaching routines onto those.

The problem is that the conventional scales against which we can measure these are calibrated for the education system.

As a teacher, I often found myself looking in the wrong direction.

I often found myself looking for the wrong things.

It was only later that I saw what had gone on.

Appendix 1

Coursework and marks: A student perspective

Benefits of using computers: a question and some student responses

Question

Your friend has written to you, asking whether it is worth learning to use a computer in order to do homework. Write a reply based upon what you think. Here are some points that might be worth including in your reply:

> whether homework done on the computer scores more marks;
> the subjects that are most worth doing on the computer;
> the best program(s) to use;
> the amount of work that you have to do in class compared with the amount of work you have to do at home.

Responses

Year 9

It won't get you extra marks for content, you may get some for presentation. It may be possible, though, to pick up extra marks if you use a special program like Encarta 95 ... an easily operated, vast encyclopaedia with many facts and lots of information. At home it will help improve research skills and speed up the time doing it, so you can get more written content in your work.

Now I use my computer for all the work I do apart from Maths and things like that. I can draw on my computer, make music, listen to music, write stories, look up words to find a meaning for it like a dictionary, print out any work I want for homework. I think it makes homework a lot easier because of all the different programs.

The only bad point of doing your homework on a computer is that you tend to find you have a lot more homework as you cannot write things up in lesson. ... PS Make sure you get some good games etc. Doom2 is an excellent game.

I have a CD-ROM at home and find it very useful when doing projects ... could result in getting better marks as you have more info on the topic.

... if you don't have a computer and your handwriting is not too good then you could lose marks for being untidy...

I find it a lot quicker to write up on a computer, and I find it much easier to write as it all just flows out.

At home, I have a PC, bought originally for my Dad when he was self-employed, but it is only a 286 and cannot run that much. We use WordPerfect 5 for DOS. I normally get better grades because it is neater and I can go into more depth. It also saves drafting.

The amount of time spent on homework is still the same but when on computer you end up doing more detailed work and more of it too.

... I use Encarta at home it's cool ...

Computers are the future they are quick and easy.

Once you have finished and the teacher asks you to add or do it again you can say "OK" without a face.

My advice to you is "Buy a computer." you won't believe how handy they are ... it also helps you get better marks because it looks good and worth reading even if what's written inside is not really that good.

... the writing is smaller when you print it out ... you have to write more so you get a better mark.

I think that no matter what teachers say about you not getting any extra marks for the work being printed, a well-presented piece of typed work with (obviously) no crossings-out and no spelling mistakes can make a teacher go "Wow!" as soon as they see it.

Year 10

On my PC we have AmiPro, for a word-processing package and Lotus 1-2-3 as a spreadsheet program. I use the computer to word process assignments as my handwriting is very messy. Also because it is easy to change things, and move things around. On AmiPro there is also a Thesaurus, a spell-check and a grammar check, which I think improves my work.

... they can get you marks for presentation, spelling, punctuation and sentence structure. If I do a draft and want to change it , it is quicker and easier than scribbling and making the paper messy, so you can read it.

Computers are expensive but if you didn't have one you probably would be degraded because of it in later life.

It also makes it easier for the teacher to read so I think it helps them when marking too. I do find that I do get better marks when I use a computer for my work but I think this is because when doing work on the computer you think about what you're doing more.

Although your work doesn't look as much on a computer it is still the same content and is easy for the teachers to work on and read.

Computers can make homework need a lot more time, even if you're very good at using them, because you end up spending a lot of time tweaking your work. The end product can look very good, especially with expert use. Spellchecks and automatic language aids such as Thesaurus help your writing. Computers with reference software, such as "Encarta" are great for research. AmiPro2 is the best word processor/d.t.p. program in the world. Apart from AmiPro3. You can also sharpen up your brains playing games such as Tetris and Doom.

Year 12

Computers are rubbish - drug of the nation blah, blah, blah. etc., etc.
(From a student who, throughout his school career, had strenuously resisted any suggestion that learning to use a computer may benefit him.)

Appendix 2

What is the Mind?   How does it work?

What makes us human: a question and some student responses

Question

Responses from the students were elicited by asking them to write an explanation based on the prompt:

Visitors from another Galaxy are approaching Earth.   They are (not unnaturally) interested in us.   You have been asked to contribute to inter-galactic understanding and explain what makes us Human.

Your task is to explain:
what the human Mind is;
how it works.

Responses

Student comments have been arranged thematically and in terms of student cohort.

The Mind as the control agent of the body

The human Mind is a kind of machine, it helps us to move around.

(Boy, Year 7.)

Its purpose is to control the human body.

(Boy, Year 7.)

The Mind is the human instruction manual. It is the controller of your body. It is more powerful than a computer or anything else known to man.

(Boy, Year 7.)

The Mind is something in our head that controls what we do and what we remember.

(Boy, Year 7.)

The human Mind is the part that controls the body.

(Boy, Year 8.)

The human Mind is complex. It physically works by giving instructions to the rest of the body. It is the control centre of a human being.

(Girl, Year 8.)

You control the human Mind and what you do is your business.

(Boy, Year 8.)

The human Mind is what humans use to do things.

(Boy, Year 8.)

The human Mind is a collection of thought and emotions which controls the body.

(Boy, Year 9.)

It controls the body and determines what sort of person you are.

(Girl, Year 9.)

Everything we see, hear, witness or feel is locked in our Minds. These things are then followed by a reaction, and the whole process is repeated.

(Girl, Year 9.)

The human Mind well, scientifically it is the control centre of the body, a large mass of tissue which has cells that are interconnected by pathways along which electrical impulses flow, but as humans we know that there is a lot more to it than that.

(Boy, Year 9.)

The human Mind works in combination with the brain. Your brain tells you your knowledge and your Mind thinks about it. The Mind is not a physical thing, but in a way it is.

(Boy, Year 9.)

Human behaviour cannot be predicted, as it is not controlled by anyone, just the Mind.

(Girl, Year 9.)

The Mind as synonymous with brain

The human Mind is called a brain, it controls our thoughts and feelings.

(Girl, Year 7.)

The Mind and brain are not the same, the brain is an object, the Mind isn't.

(Girl, Year 7.)

The brain (Mind) works by sending signals through nerves which tell a certain part of the body to function.

(Girl, Year 7.)

The human Mind is the brain.

(Girl, Year 7.)

The human Mind is not a 3D thing so it can not be touched. It is part of our brain.

(Boy, Year 7.)

Our human Mind is the brain and the brain, if you think about it, is like a control that operates the rest of the body.

(Boy, Year 7.)

Your Mind is controlled by your brain and whatever that's thinking.

(Boy, Year 8.)

The Mind is actually part of our brains, our brains are what do all of the thinking (like the processor of a PC) but the Mind is where all the memories of the past are stored.

(Boy, Year 8.)

The Mind works because of your brain. The brain gives you thoughts and that's what we call the Mind.

(Boy, Year 8.)

The human Mind exists in the brain, although it does not exist, if you know what I mean.

(Boy, Year 10.)

The Mind as the process of thinking

The human Mind is a thing in our head, it helps us think before we do anything.

(Girl, Year 7.)

…we are free to do and think what we want most of the time.

(Girl, Year 7.)

The human Mind uses information from the past to help decide the future and works on early experiences.

(Girl, Year 7.)

The human Mind is the centre of our thoughts.

(Girl, Year 7.)

It works by thinking ... when somebody comes up and asks you, you can say it quick and sharp without trying to think what it is or trying to stand there mumbling in your head.

(Boy, Year 7.)

Your Mind is where all your logic is, but no feelings.

(Boy, Year 7.)

The human Mind is the thinking chamber of the human body.

(Girl, Year 7.)

The Mind is the thing that thinks.

(Boy, Year 8.)

Your Mind is what you think.

(Boy, Year 8.)

A thinking place full of emotions, it makes decisions and controls your feelings. It is controlled by your thoughts.

(Boy, Year 8.)

It allows you to think privately to yourself.

(Girl, Year 8.)

The human Mind allows people to thing and act for themselves. It is a message centre for all your thoughts.

(Girl, Year 8.)

The Mind is a complex thing which makes you think, it works with the brain. The Mind, in a way, dictates the things you do or think.

(Girl, Year 8.)

The Mind allows us to produce ideas, to work out things, the Mind is helping me to decide what I am writing down this very minute, in fact.

(Girl, Year 8.)

I think the human Mind is like your own private library, it is where you can think about anything you want.

(Boy, Year 8.)

The Mind is not the visible part of the brain but is the part in which all the problems and judgements are made.

(Girl, Year 9.)

It works by gathering thoughts and processing them through the body.

(Girl, Year 9.)

It is how you perceive reality and life.

(Boy, Year 10.)

It doesn't exist in the physical state, but it handles the thought matrix.

(Boy, Year 12.)

The Mind as storage; memory

The human Mind is like a memory bank which stores all your memories.

(Boy, Year 7.)

The Mind is a thing which we use to think of things that we need, have or want and keeps everything in order and in the right place.

(Boy, Year 7.)

I think that the human Mind is a big roll of paper and a pen inside your head that never ends and the pen writes down anything you want on the paper.

(Girl, Year 7.)

The human Mind stores information, memories, intelligence and most things that happen to a human.

(Girl, Year 7.)

I think the human Mind is like a big encyclopedia. It stores knowledge.

(Girl, Year 7.)

(It) is split into sections for each of our five senses and a section for storing information and controlling the body…

(Girl, Year 7.)

Our Mind takes all our memories and helps us all the time until we die.

(Boy, Year 8.)

It's like an organizer, you remember everything in there.

(Girl, Year 9.)

The Mind as emotions, feelings

Your Mind is different from your brain because your Mind goes on feelings and thoughts. Your brain is controlled by cells but your Mind is free.

(Girl, Year 7.)

Some of us have a Mind where we are very emotional but some have very strong Minds and can 'fight back' not flood into tears.

(Girl, Year 7.)

It can make illusions seem real.

(Girl, Year 7.)

Humans have emotions which control our temperament.

(Boy, Year 7.)

It helps people think about their feelings.

(Girl, Year 8.)

The human Mind is different to the brain because the Mind deals with emotions and that sort of thing and the brain deals with sending messages to different parts of your body.

(Boy, Year 8.)

It gives you feelings, say if you've fallen in love or someone hurts you.

(Girl, Year 8.)

The brain helps you see, hear and smell, but the Mind has feelings and thoughts.

(Boy, Year 9.)

The Mind as ethical standards

Also it is our conscience telling us what to do.

(Girl, Year 7.)

It can determine right from wrong ... it sets a person's own morals to live by.

(Girl, Year 12.)

The Mind as an individual's identity

The human Mind is our body. It makes us who we are and what we are.

(Boy, Year 7.)

If we didn't have a Mind we would not be human.

(Girl, Year 7.)

It gives you a personality that makes you an individual in your own Mind.

(Boy, Year 7.)

It is what makes you. It's your personality, your feelings, your views.

(Boy, Year 7.)

I think the human Mind is whatever you want it to be.

(Girl, Year 8.)

I think it's like where your personality is.

(Girl, Year 8.)

Your character and personality come from your Mind.

(Boy, Year 8.)

The human Mind is what makes us individual or special. If you took away our Minds we would all be the same - like robots.

(Boy, Year 8.)

The human Mind is the thing inside that makes us have a unique personality.

(Girl, Year 8.)

We cannot be human without our Minds, but we can be human if we don't have something else.

(Girl, Year 8.)

I think the human Mind is like a second self. You know what you are doing but you can only think.

(Girl, Year 9.)

Without our Mind, we are nothing apart from raw materials. A Mind makes us what we are.

(Girl, Year 9.)

The human Mind is a genetic masterpiece. It is unique in everyone and everything and operates the thoughts of everyone. It cannot be replicated.

(Boy, Year 9.)

We are not like computers because computers can't change what they do unless they are programmed to, but we can change what we do whenever we want. I think that we are the person that our Mind is.

(Boy, Year 9.)

It seems a very unusual thing to say, but your Mind is you and who you are.

(Girl, Year 9.)

The human Mind is a construct of our inner emotions and deep thoughts.

(Boy, Year 10.)

Images which you can see in your head but not necessarily through your eyes, as you normally see.

(Boy, Year 10.)

The human Mind is what makes us individuals, but what links us as humans. It is what helps us perceive the world as individuals.

(Girl, Year 12.)

The Mind as a computer

The Mind is like a computer because it stores lots of information in its memory database and it has many output devices like speaking, moving etc. It works by taking in a huge quantity of information.

(Boy, Year 7.)

It is like an on board Apple Mac (computer). It stores memory. It learns things.

(Boy, Year 7.)

It works like a big computer and we humans only use about 10%.

(Boy, Year 7.)

It works like a computer, you can't get information from it without someone putting it in, like disks.

(Boy, Year 7.)

The human Mind works like a computer, we input things and output things.

(Boy, Year 8.)

The Mind is like a computer and our nervous system is like the wires we have a hard drive (memory) and many programs (moods) but only one screen personality.

(Boy, Year 8.)

You could describe the Mind as a computer also full of information.

(Girl, Year 8.)

The human Mind and brain is slightly like a very sophisticated computer.

(Girl, Year 8.)

It is like a computer, it stores images as well as thoughts and feelings.

(Boy, Year 8.)

Your Mind is your own imaginative personal computer.

(Boy, Year 9.)

Like a computer where you type things in and the human does it. The Mind is like the Internet a bit - now that's amazing.

(Boy, Year 9.)

I think that the human Mind is like a massive computer that stores loads of information and has a massive memory. When you are born it is switched on and when you die it switches off.

(Boy, Year 9.)

Metaphysical concepts of the Mind

I think when you die you can never turn off you become something else but you just don't remember your past life.

(Girl, Year 8.)

It's the untouched part of your body, it's your self-conscious.

(Boy, Year 8.)

The Mind is a deep psychic connection between body and brain.

(Boy, Year 9.)

An inner voice

The Mind is where a human's thought are transferred from everything in a human's brain to a silent voice in the human's head. The silent voice or Mind is speaking all the time.

(Boy, Year 8.)

You have conversations with your Mind and it helps you decide things.

(Girl, Year 8.)

It's like your inner self, a voice that is telling you what to do and how to live.

(Girl, Year 9.)

It is a voice within, and is active all the time: it is a voice within a person telling them things that no-one else should know.

(Girl, Year 12.)

The soul

Some people believe that you have a soul, this might be part of the Mind and some people believe that when you die this part of you rises to heaven. The Mind can play a great part in religion.

(Girl, Year 8.)

Your Mind is not an organ you could never find it. Your Mind is the same as your soul, it goes to heaven.

(Girl, Year 8.)

I believe that the human Mind is our soul … our soul never dies, and if the soul doesn't die, the Mind doesn't, either.

(Girl, Year 9.)

This could be said to be a soul, without which the human would just be an empty body with no personality.

(Boy, Year 9.)

The human Mind is our sort of soul.

(Boy, Year 9.)

God/supernatural

The human Mind is part of God. It is his way of controlling human beings.

(Girl, Year 10.)

The human Mind is the control station to your body. God is the Lord of the control station. If God is not believed in the Mind has another controller.

(Girl, Year 10.)

A myth, dream, abstraction

I think that the human Mind is like a dream machine and when you do not dream the dreams and the body stop.

(Girl, Year 9.)

The Mind is capable of dreaming up many wonderful things which don't have to exist.

(Boy, Year 9.)

The human Mind is a dream.

(Boy, Year 9.)

The human Mind is built to succeed, every human being, no matter what age, sex or colour has a dream and a goal. As soon as we were born we were trying to reach that dream, and our aim in life is to succeed. Without the human Mind it is impossible to have the ability to do that.

(Girl, Year 10.)

Appendix 3

How do you learn?   Some student comments

When I'm taught people tell me the things I am learning, but when I am learning I do it myself.

(Girl, Year 7.)

If you are made to learn something you find it kind of boring, but if you want to learn something, it sort of gives you an independence that makes you feel good.

(Girl, Year 7.)

You're taught by listening and you learn by practice.

(Girl, Year 8.)

When you want to learn you try harder but when you have to learn it is harder.

(Girl, Year 7.)

Teachers shout at you. I don't shout at myself.

(Boy, Year 7.)

Teachers tell you off and disturb me (sic) education time.

(Boy, Year 7.)

They talk, we listen.

(Boy, Year 9.)

We don't 'have' to learn things, but pressure is put on us to learn things as we have an easier time if we do.

(Boy, Year 9.)

Learning is something you do for yourself. Being taught is something the teacher does for you.

(Girl, Year 9.)

When you're taught they tell you and you still don't know. But when you learn you know what it is.

(Boy, Year 10.)

(I learn things by) …experience and studying. Doing it!   You learn at your own rate but you are taught at someone else's pace.

(Boy, Year 10.)

People will say something and if it makes sense to me I remember it. My brain is quite organised into sections and new facts usually slot in nicely where they should be. If I don't understand things first time then I usually find a pictorial explanation helps.

(Boy, Year 10.)

I learn things through spider diagrams, reading text then writing it down in notes, pictures and tables.

(Girl, Year 10.)

You have to learn how to soap them up, clean them and then put them back together again after you've cleaned them. Different types of horses use different types of tack. It's all part of learning to ride.

(Girl, Year 10.)

I have learned how to help children … put makeup on and shave my legs etc. I have learned how to change the style of my hair … how to horse ride.

(Girl, Year 10.)

Perseverance and practice are essential to most learning processes, and although the sense of achievement may be greater when learning something through choice, the determination is equally strong in learning an essential skill or fact.

(Boy, Year 12.)

I display all the things I need to know on my bedroom wall. When I learn I am alone with all the info. displayed.

(Girl, Year 12.)

When I want to learn I push harder for information. When I have to I just take the information in. I learn things through different note styles, such as spider diagrams, bullet points and using a dictaphone.

(Girl, Year 12.)

Bibliography

Abbot, C. (1998), Unpublished research, London, King's College.

Barthes, R. (1982), *A Barthes Reader,* (ed.), Sontag, S. London, Jonathan Cape.

Bateson, M. (1972), *Steps to an ecology of Mind,* New York, Ballantine Books.

Baudrillard, J. (1987), *Forget Foucault,* New York, Semiotext(e).

BBC News Online UK, (02.04.98), *Teachers need IT training,* http://www.bbc.co.uk/news

BBC News Online UK, (18.11.98), *Pupils denied Internet access,* http://www.bbc.co.uk/news

Belson, W. (1978), *Television Violence and the Adolescent Boy,* Farnborough, Saxon House.

Beishuizen, J., Stoutjesdijk, E. (1999), Study strategies in a computer assisted study environment, *Learning and Instruction,* Vol. 9, No. 3, pp. 281-301.

Birnbaum, L. (1991), *Three Critical Essays on Language and Representation,* Northwestern University, The Institute for the Learning Sciences.

Blair, A. (1998), Announcement of government spending on information technology in schools, *The Times,* 07.11.98, *The Independent,* 07.11.98.

Blumenthal, W. (1986), *The effects of computer instruction on low achieving children's academic self-beliefs and performance,* Nova University.

Bourdieu, P. (1986), The forms of capital, In: *Handbook of Theory and Research for the Sociology of Education,* (ed.), Richardson, J.G., New York, Greenwood Press.

Bourdieu, P. (1993), *The Field of Cultural Production,* Cambridge, Polity Press.

British Computer Society (1997), ICT in Schools, *Computer Bulletin Supplement.*

Bruner, J. S. (1966), *Towards a Theory of Instruction,* Cambridge, MIT Press.

Bruner, J. S. (1974), *Beyond the Information Given,* London, George Allen and Unwin Ltd.

Bruner, Oliver and Greenfield (1966), *Studies in cognitive growth,* New York, Wiley.

Buckingham, D. (1996), *Moving Images: Understanding Children's Emotional Responses to Television,* Manchester, Manchester University Press.

Chomsky, N. (1972), *Language and Mind,* Harcourt Brace New York.

Clements, D.H., Gullo , D.F. (1984), Effects of computer programming on young children's cognition, *Journal of Educational Psychology,* Vol. 76, pp. 1051-1058.

Clements, D., Meredith, J. (1985), *Research on Logo: Effects and Efficacy,* State University of New York at Buffalo.

Clements, D.H., Nastasi, B.K. (1985), Effects of computer environments on social-emotional development: Logo and computer-assisted instruction, *Computers in the Schools*, Vol. 2, Nos. 2-3, pp. 11-31.

Clements, D.H., Nastasi, B.K. (1988), Social and cognitive interactions in educational computer environments, *American Educational Research Journal*, Vol. 25, pp. 87-106.

Clynes, M., Kline, N. (1960), In: *The Cyborg Handbook* (ed.), Gray, Figueroa-Sarriera, Mentor, S. (1995), London, Routledge.

Collins, R., Curran, J., Garnham, N., Scannel, P., Schlesinger, P., Sparks, C. (eds), (1986), *Media, Culture And Society: A Critical Reader*, London, Sage Publications.

Cox, M.J. (1997), *The effects of Information Technology on Students' Motivation*, NCET, Coventry.

Cullingford, C. (1984), *Children and Television*, Aldershot, Gower.

DfEE (1997), *Excellence in Schools*, White Paper on standards in education, Cm3681, London, Department for Education and Employment (DfEE).

Donaldson, M. (1987), *Children's Minds*, London, Fontana.

Dwyer, D. (1994), Apple classrooms of Tomorrow: What we've learned *Educational Leadership*, Vol. 51, No. 7, p. 4.

Eco, U. (1976), A *Theory of Semiotics*, Bloomington: Indiana University Press/London: Macmillan.

Eco, U. ([1986] 1987), *Travels in Hyper-Reality*, London, Picador.

Elliott, C. D. (1992), *The Affective Reasoner: A Process Model of Emotions in a Multi-agent System*, Technical Report No. 32 Northwestern University, The Institute for the Learning Sciences.

Felder, M., Soloman, B. (1998), *Learning Styles and Strategies*, North Carolina State University, http://www2.ncsu.edu.

Foucault, M. (1983), *This Is Not A Pipe*, University of California Press.

Gardner, H. (1983), *Frames of Mind, The Theory of Multiple Intelligences*, London, Heinemann.

Gardner, H. (1993), *The Unschooled Mind, How Children Think and How Schools Should Teach*, London, Fontana.

Garfinkel, H. (1967), *Studies in Ethnomethodology*, Englewood Cliffs, Prentice-Hall.

Gopnik, A., Melzoff, A.N. (1997), *Words, Thoughts and Theories*, Cambridge, MA, MIT Press.

Gray, C.H. (1995), *The Cyborg Handbook,* London, Routledge.

Griffith, M., Miller, H., Gillespie, T., Sparrow, P. (1999), Internet usage and internet 'addiction' in students and its implications for learning, *Journal of Computer Assisted Learning* Vol. 15, No. 1, pp. 89-90.

Gurevitch, M., Bennet, T., Curran, C., Woollacott, J. (eds), (1982), *Culture, Society and the Media*, London, Methuen.

Hagmann, S., Mayer, R., Nenniger, P. (1998), Using structural theory to make a word-processing manual more understandable, *Learning and Instruction*, Vol. 8, No. 1, pp. 19-35.

Haraway, D. (1985), The Cyborg Manifesto, Science, Technology and Socialist-Feminism in the late Twentieth Century, In: *Simians, Cyborgs and Women* (1991), London Free Association Books.

Hawkes, T. (1977), *Structuralism and Semiotics,* Methuen, London.

Himmelweit, H.T., Oppenheim, A.N., Vince, P. (1958), *Television And The Child, An empirical study of the effect of television on the young,* London, The Nuffield Foundation.

Hodge, R., Tripp. D. (1986), *Children and Television, A Semiotic Approach,* Cambridge, Polity Press.

Hodges, M.E., Sasnett, R.M., (1990), *Multimedia Computing: Case studies from MIT project Athena,* Adison-Wesley, MA, USA.

Horner, C.M., Maddux, C.D. (1985) The effect of Logo on attributions toward success, *Computers in the Schools,* Vol. 2, Nos. 2-3: pp. 45-54.

Hughes, M., Macleod, H. (1986), Part II: Using Logo with very young children, In: *Cognition and Computers: Studies in Learning,* Lawler, et al. (eds), Chichester, Ellis Horwood.

Information Technology and Education Programme:

ITE/12/86 Lewis, R. *Some Aspects of the Classroom Processes.*

ITE/18/86 Moore, J.L. *Computer Education Activities and Pupils' Attitudes to Computers.*

ITE/13/86 Lewis, R. *Teacher-Fellowship Research Programme.*

ITE/20/87 Saunders, M., Machell, J. *CBT Evaluation Techniques and Processes – An Interim report.*

ITE/24/88 Lewis, R. (ed.), *DES/ESRC Teacher Fellows 1986/7: - abstracts of research.*

ITE/25a/88 Lewis, R. (ed.), *Research in Progress.*

ITE/25b/88 Lewis, R. (ed.), *Research in Progress.*

ITE/26/88 Lewis, R. (ed.), *Learning through Microworlds.*

ITE/28a/88 Wellington, J., *Policies and Trends in IT and Education.*

Information Technology in Education Research Programme (InTER), 1988-93.

InTER/2/88 Cumming, G. (ed.), *Artificial Intelligence Applications to Learning and Training.*

InTER/3/1988 Eraut, M., Holes, C. *Groupwork with Computers.*

InTER/4/1988 Driver, R., Scanlon, E. *Conceptual Change in Science.*

InTER/6/1988 Macdonald, B., Stronach, I. *The Independent Policy Evaluation.*

InTER/7/1988 Lewis, R., Mace, T.D. *Support Tools for Authoring.*

InTER/9a/1989 Bryson, M. *A guide to the Electronic services.*

InTER/10/1989 Rymaszewski, R. *Information Technology and Language Development.*

InTER/11/1989 Rhodes, V. *Barriers to Innovation.*

InTER/12/1989 Hodgson, V., Lewis, R., McConnel, D., *Information Technology-based Open Learning – a Study Report.*

InTER/13/1989 Lewis, R., Mace, T., *Authoring Tools for simulation-based CBT – an interim project report.*

InTER/14/1990 Boots, M. *Research in Progress.*

InTER/15/1990 Rhodes, V., Cox, M. *Current Practice and Policies for using Computers in Primary Schools: implications for training.*

InTER/16/1990 Cumming, G., Lewis, R. *Exploration and Reasoning – a seminar report.*

InTER/17/1990 STAC Project Team *Supporting Technology across the Curriculum.*

InTER/18/1990 McMahon, H., O'Neill, B. *Capturing Dialogue in Learning.*

Inhelder, B., Piaget, J. (1958), *The Growth of Logical Thinking from Childhood to Adolescence*, London, Routledge and Kegan Paul.

Jaglom, L., Gardner, H. (1981), Decoding the worlds of television, In: *Children and Television* (1986), Polity Press, Cambridge.

Jameson, F. (1991), *Postmodernism, Or, The Cultural Logic of Late Capitalism*, Durham, Duke University Press.

Jarvela, S., Niemivirta, M. (1999), The changes in learning theory and the topicality of the recent research on motivation, *Research Dialogue in Learning and Instruction*, Vol. 1, No. 2, pp. 57-65.

Kapa, E. (1999), Problem-Solving, planning ability and sharing processes with LOGO, *Journal of Computer Assisted Learning* Vol. 15, No. 1, pp. 73-84.

Kaplan, E.A., (1987), *Rocking Around The Clock: Music Television, Postmodernism, and Consumer Culture*, London, Methuen.

Kass, A.M. (1990), *Developing Creative Hypotheses By Adapting Explanations*, Northwestern University, The Institute for the Learning Sciences.

Knowles, M. (1970), *The Modern Practice of Adult Education: Andragogy vs, Pedagogy*, New York, Association Press.

Kolb, D. (1984), *Experiential Learning: Experience as the Source of Learning and Development*, New Jersey, Prentice Hall.

Latour, B. (1993), *We have never been modern*, New York, Harvard University Press.

Leask, M., Pachler, N. (eds), (1999), *Learning to teach using ICT in the secondary school*, London, Routledge.

Leiber, J. (1991), *An Invitation to Cognitive Science*, Oxford, Basil Blackwell.

Levi Strauss, C. (1962), *The Savage Mind*, Oxford, Oxford University Press.

Levinson, P. (1997), *The soft edge*, London, Routledge.

Longman (1997), *PC ownership survey*, Cambridge, Longman Logotron.

Lovink, G. (1995), *The Media Gesture of Data Dandyism* CTHEORY Theory, Technology and Culture, Concordia, Canada http://www.ctheory.com/ (27.11.1996)

Lyons, J. (1981), *Language and Linguistics*, Cambridge, University of Cambridge Press.

McKinsey and Company (1997), *The Future of Information Technology in UK Schools*, London, McKinsey and Co.

McLuhan, M. (1964), *Understanding Media*, London, Penguin.

McQuail, D. (1969), *Towards a Sociology of Mass Communications*, London, Macmillan.

McQuail, D. (1987), *Mass Communication Theory*, (2nd edn.), London, Sage.

McQuail, D. (ed.), (1972), *Sociology of Mass Communications*, Harmondsworth, Penguin Books.

McQuail, D., Windahl, S. (1981), *Communication Models for the Study of Mass Communications*, London, Longman.

McShane, J. (1991), *Cognitive development: An Information Processing Approach*, Oxford, Basil Blackwell.

Matthew, G.B. (1994), *The Philosophy of Childhood*, Harvard University Press Cambridge, MA.

Maturana, H.R. (1970), Biology of Cognition In: Maturana and Varela: *Autopoiesis and Cognition*, Reidel Dordrecht.

Monteith, M. (1996), IT: home and school *Microscope* (48), Autumn 1996.

Morley, D. (1986), *Family Television: Cultural Power and Domestic Leisure*, London, Comedia.

OFSTED (1998), *Secondary Education 1993-97, A Review of Secondary Schools in England*, Office for Standards in Education (OFSTED), London.

Oppenheimer, T. (1997), The Computer Delusion, *The Atlantic Monthly*, July, Vol. 280, No. 1, pp. 45-62.

Papert, S. (1980), *Mindstorms Children, Computers and Powerful Ideas*, Brighton, The Harvester Press.

Papert, S. (1996), Looking at Technology through School-Colored Spectacles, *The Electronic Policy Network*, http://epn.org/conferen/spapert.html. (10.02.99.)

Pea, R.D. (1992), *Practices of Distributed Intelligence and Designs for Education*, Technical Report No. 21,The Institute for the Learning Sciences.

Pea, R.D., Gomez, L.M. (1992), *Distributed Multimedia Learning Environments: Why and How?* Technical Report No. 25 Northwestern University, The Institute for the Learning Sciences.

Piaget, J. (1953), *The Origin of Intelligence in the Child*, London, Routledge and Kegan Paul.

Piaget, J. (1972), *The Principles of Genetic Epistemology*, London, Routledge and Kegan Paul.

Piaget, J. (1968), *Structuralism*, London, Routledge and Kegan Paul.

Porter, J. (1998), A Trip Down Memory Lane, *Wired* 6,04: Electric Word 10/06/98 http://www.wired.com (10/06/98).

Preston C., Harris S. (1993), *Software in Schools*, Slough, NFER.

Preston C., Cox, M., Cox, K. (2000), *Teachers as Innovators, An evaluation of the motivation of teachers to use information and communication technologies*, London, MirandaNet.

Randall, B., Ringland, G., Wulf, W. (1994), *Software 2000: a View of the Future*, Brussels/Stevenage Commission of the European Communities/ ICL.

Ricoeur, P. (1978), *The Rule of Metaphor*, London, Routledge and Kegan Paul.

Robinson, M. (1997), *Children Reading Print and Television*, London, The Falmer Press.

Salomon, G. (1998), Novel Constructivist Learning Environments and Novel Technologies: Some Issues To Be Concerned With, *Research Dialogue in Learning and Instruction*, Vol. 1, No. 1, pp. 3-12.

Sanger, J., Willson, J., Davies, B., Whittaker, R. (1997), *Young Children, Videos and Computer Games*, London, The Falmer Press.

Sapir, E. (1921), *Language*, New York, Harcourt Brace.

Sapir, E. (1947), *Selected Writings in Language, Culture and Personality*, Berkeley and Los Angeles, University of California Press.

Schank, R.C., Jona, M.Y. (1990), *Empowering the Student: New Perspectives on the Design of Teaching Systems*, Evanston, Il, Northwestern University, The Institute for the Learning Sciences.

Schank, R.C. (1990), *Teaching Architectures*, Technical Report No. 3 Evanston, Il, Northwestern University, The Institute for the Learning Sciences.

Schank, R.C., Edelson, D.J. (1990), *A Role for AI in Education: Using Technology to Reshape Education*, Technical Report No. 1 Evanston, Il, Northwestern University, The Institute for the Learning Sciences.

Schostak, J. (1988), *Breaking into the Curriculum: the Impact of Information Technology on Schooling*, London, Methuen.

Searle, J.R. (1995), *The Construction of Social Reality*, Harmondsworth, Allen Lane.

Searle, J.R. (1992), *The Rediscovery of the Mind*, Cambridge, Ma, The MIT Press.

Seigel, L., Brainerd, C. (eds) (1978), *Alternatives to Piaget, Critical Essays on the Theory*, London, Academic Press.

Severin, W.J., Tankard, J.W. (1997), *Communication Theories: Origins, Methods, and Uses in the Mass Media*, London, Addison Wesley.

Shneiderman, B. Human Interface, The Next Accomplishment For Computers in: *Perspective (NCR)*, Vol. 3, No. 4 University of Maryland Human-Computer Interaction Laboratory.

Shneiderman, B. (1991), Education by Engagement and Construction: A Strategic Education Initiative for a Multi-media Renewal of American Education in: *Sociomedia, Multimedia, Hypermedia, and the Social Construction of Knowledge*, Ed. Barret, E., Cambridge, MA, The MIT Press.

Shneiderman, B. (1993), Engagement and Construction: Educational Strategies for the Post-TV Era, *Journal of Computing in Higher Education*, Vol. 4, No. 2, pp. 106-116.

Somekh, B. (1986), In: Schostak, J. (1988), *Breaking into the Curriculum: the Impact of Information Technology on Schooling*, London, Methuen.

Somekh, B., Davis, N. (1991), Toward a Pedagogy for Information Technology, *The Curriculum Journal*, Vol. 2, No. 2, pp. 153-170.

Somekh, B., Davis, N. (eds), (1997), *Using Information Technology Effectively in Teaching and Learning, Studies in Pre-service and In-service Teacher Education*, London, Routledge.

Stevenson, J. (1998), Performance of the Cognitive Holding Power Questionnaire in School, *Learning and Instruction*, Vol. 8, No. 5, pp. 393-411.

Sussex University, A study of more than 20 teleworkers and their families, Science and Policy Research Unit, 1994.

Turkle, S. (1995), *Life on the Screen, Identity in the Age of the Internet*, New York, Simon and Schuster.

Underwood, J., Underwood, G. (1990), *Computers and Learning: Helping children acquire thinking skills*, Oxford, Basil Blackwell.

Veblen, T. (1899), *The Theory of the Leisure Class*, New York, Macmillan.

Virilio, P. (1995), Red Alert in Cyberspace From: *Le Monde Diplomatique* August 1995, Translated in: *Radical Philosophy* 74, December 1995, London Central Books.

Vygotsky, L.S. (1962), *Thought and Language*, Cambridge, MIT Press.

Watson, D. (1987), *Developing CAL: Computers in the Curriculum*, London, Harper and Rowe.

Watson, D. (1993), *IMPACT – An Evaluation of the IMPACT of the Information Technology on Children's Achievements in Primary and Secondary Schools*, London, Kings College.

Wertsch, J.V. (1998), *Mind as Action*, Oxford, Oxford University Press.

Whorf, B.L. (1956), *Language, Thought and Reality*, Cambridge, MIT Press.

Winograd, T., Flores, F. (1988), *Understanding Computers and Cognition*, Reading, Ma, Addison Wesley.

Index